THE VIRTUAL ADVISOR

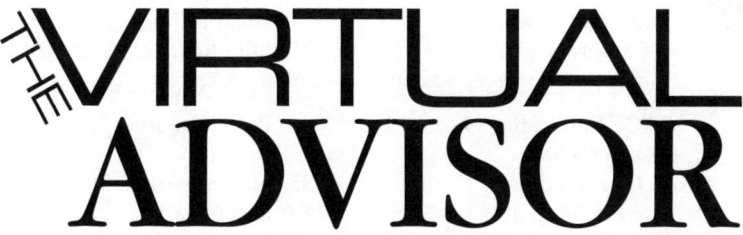

Successful Strategies for Getting Into Graduate School in Psychology

Greg J. Neimeyer
University of Florida

Diane Stevenson
University of Florida

Los Angeles • London • New Delhi • Singapore

Copyright © 2008 by SAGE Publications, Inc.

All rights reserved. No part of this book may be reproduced or utilized in any form or by any means, electronic or mechanical, including photocopying, recording, or by any information storage and retrieval system, without permission in writing from the publisher.

For information:

SAGE Publications, Inc.
2455 Teller Road
Thousand Oaks,
  California 91320
E-mail: order@sagepub.com

SAGE Publications Ltd.
1 Oliver's Yard
55 City Road
London EC1Y 1SP
United Kingdom

SAGE Publications India Pvt. Ltd.
B 1/I 1 Mohan Cooperative
  Industrial Area
Mathura Road, New Delhi 110 044
India

SAGE Publications Asia-Pacific
  Pte. Ltd.
33 Pekin Street #02-01
Far East Square
Singapore 048763

Printed in the United States of America

Library of Congress Cataloging-in-Publication Data

Neimeyer, Greg J.
  The virtual advisor: successful strategies for getting into graduate school in psychology/Greg J. Neimeyer, Diane Stevenson.
       p. cm.
  Includes bibliographical references and index.
  ISBN 978-1-4129-6417-3 (paper)

  1. Psychology—Study and teaching. 2. Counseling—Study and teaching. 3. Universities and colleges—Entrance requirements. 4. Universities and colleges—Graduate work—Admission. I. Stevenson, Diane. II. Title.

BF77.N45 2008
150.71′173—dc22   2008004781

This book is printed on acid-free paper.

08 09 10 11 12 10 9 8 7 6 5 4 3 2 1

Acquisitions Editor:	Kassie Graves
Editorial Assistant:	Veronica Novak
Production Editor:	Laureen A. Shea
Copy Editor:	Kathy Anne Savadel
Typesetter:	C&M Digitals (P) Ltd.
Proofreader:	Jenifer Kooiman
Cover Designer:	Edgar Abarca
Marketing Manager:	Carmel Schrire

Contents

Acknowledgments	vii
1. Introducing Your Virtual Advisor	1
2. Developing Your Vita	7
Making Structure Out of Chaos	9
Constructing Your Vita	10
Framing Your Picture	13
3. Crafting Your Personal Statement	27
Approaching the Task: General Comments	28
The Before: Research!	30
The After: Edit! Revise! Rewrite! Reconsider! Start Over! Write a Second Draft!	32
Why Is Writing a Personal Statement Such an Unpleasant Experience? Getting Started	33
Don'ts	43
Do's	45
Structuring the Personal Statement	48
This and That	51
Style: Writing Vibrant, Lively Prose	53
4. Securing Your Letters of Recommendation	63
To Waive or Not to Waive: That Is the Option	71
How to Maximize the Impact of Your Letters	72
Turning a Letter From Lukewarm to Red Hot	72
The Thumbnail Sketch	73
Timing	80
Putting It All Together	81
Make It Easy	81
5. Getting Into the Flow	87
About the Authors	93

Acknowledgments

The authors wish to thank all the students over the years who have contributed their experiences, their questions and answers, their successes, insights, and examples. Special thanks to John Denton, and to Charline Simon for her help with the flowcharts.

1

Introducing Your Virtual Advisor

In This Online and Pocket Companion Program You Will Learn:

- ❖ About areas of psychology (e.g., cognitive, developmental, social, and industrial–organizational psychology)
- ❖ About careers in psychology based on type of degree
- ❖ About a PhD versus a PsyD versus an MA (or MS)
- ❖ About preparing for graduate school, inside and outside the classroom
- ❖ About "goodness of fit" and the process of applying to graduate school
- ❖ About crafting your vita, writing your personal statement, and obtaining letters of recommendation
- ❖ About interviewing

Have you ever found yourself thinking, "I only wish I knew *then* what I know *now?*" Maybe you took a new job, got a new roommate, or became involved in a relationship. Then, after some time, you found yourself wishing that you had known at the outset everything that you learned since that time—the hard way. Hindsight is 20-20, as they say. Think of all the trials, tribulations, and heartache you might have spared yourself, if only you'd known.

Well, that's what *The Virtual Advisor* is all about. It will help you ahead of time with your application to graduate school. By giving you a behind-the-scenes look at every step and stage in the process, *The Virtual Advisor* harvests all of our years and years of experience and serves them up to you *before* you apply. Think of *The Virtual Advisor* as your personal guide or coach, advising you in relation to each and every step you take in the process of graduate application, before you even begin.

The Virtual Advisor is divided into two parts: (1) *The Online Companion* and (2) *The Pocket Companion*. Each one is designed to complement and extend the other. *The Online Companion* is located at http://www.thevirtualadvisoronline.com, and you access it with your access code. Using a personal approach, *The Online Companion* provides an in-depth overview of the wide range of graduate school considerations and talks you through aspects of graduate school exploration, preparation, and application. You'll learn about different degrees, careers, and salaries in psychology, as well as how best to prepare yourself for the future of your choice. You will have lots of opportunities to assess your current position in relation to the "ideal" and to interact online as you examine yourself and explore your future. Along the way, you will meet other graduate applicants, see some of their application materials, and, in *The Online Companion,* listen to their graduate interviews, too. Because *The Online Companion* is online, it's available whenever you are, and you can return again and again to any of its modules, or download them for podcasting. So whether you are on a bike or bus, walking or running, or just sitting down with a latte, *The Online Companion* can accompany you.

The Pocket Companion is the perfect complement to *The Online Companion*. It concentrates on those features of your graduate application over which you have the most control at this time: your vita, your personal statement, and your letters of recommendation, advising you in detail exactly how best to approach each one. By giving you lots of examples and leading you through the process step by step, *The Pocket Companion* helps you craft the strongest possible graduate application materials.

Wherever you are in the process of thinking about graduate study in psychology, *The Virtual Advisor (Online Companion* and *Pocket Companion)* can help. Perhaps you are just now considering graduate school, or wondering whether you should pursue a master's degree or a doctoral degree. Maybe you have a pretty good idea that you would like to pursue a doctorate, but you are trying to sort out the differences between particular degrees—how, exactly, does a PsyD differ from a PhD?—or the differences in areas of specialization—are clinical and counseling psychology programs really *that* different? *The Virtual Advisor Online Companion* can help you with those questions in clear, straightforward, no-nonsense terms. It can help you with other questions as well, including ones you never knew you had (e.g., What is an *attrition rate*? What degrees offer licensure? Should you write a thesis?).

More than that, however, *The Virtual Advisor* actually coaches you through each component of your graduate application, inch by inch, from wherever you are to wherever you want to go. No two students ever start from exactly the same place, nor do they often have the same goal or objective. Everyone is different, so there are no hard-and-fast answers to such questions as "Should I have extensive experience in one laboratory or experience in many laboratories?" or "Should I get a PhD or a PsyD?" Your background, experiences, and credentials are distinctive, just as your goals, aspirations, and objectives are unique. And that's a good thing. Graduate schools are looking for unique people whose qualifications and career objectives fit with their distinctive offerings. A good match is vital to a successful application and, unlike "well-roundedness" in undergraduate admissions, "general excellence" is not always sufficient for admission into graduate schools in psychology. That's where your application materials come into play.

In *The Virtual Advisor*, we break your graduate application materials down into two groups: (1) objective components and (2) subjective components. *Objective* components are things that are common, descriptive, and more or less beyond your control at this point. Your transcripts, your GPA, and your GRE scores fit this bill. Yes, you may still be able to add a point or two to the first (or second) decimal place in your GPA, and you may well be able to bulk up your GRE scores by taking lots of practice tests or a GRE preparation course, but your coursework, GPA, and GRE scores are more likely to help qualify you for *further* consideration than they are to gain you admission into a graduate program. Yes, admissions committees will sit up and take notice if you were a triple major in psychology, philosophy, and physics with a 4.0 GPA, or if you crack the 1500-point threshold on the GRE, but most students do not distinguish themselves solely with these objective measures. Neither do these facts, outstanding as they are, really address what graduate programs are looking for, which is a goodness of fit between the applicants and themselves. So, although a 4.0 applicant with a GRE score of 1500 would almost assuredly be capable of completing any given graduate program, the admissions committee is still going to ask how that person would fit in, with whom he or she would work as an advisor, and what distinctive experiences, qualifications, or skills he or she would bring to the program. The objective components of your application are like the peephole in your front door: they provide a promising glimpse of the person who is outside knocking, and they may even get you invited inside. However, the question remains: *Who* is this applicant, and *what* does he or she want? The subjective components of your application can answer those questions.

The *subjective components* are all about you, distinctively. It is important to note that you have substantial control over these components and what they say about you. Into this category we place the vita, the personal statement, and the letters of recommendation (yes, you can influence the content of your letters of recommendation, and we will tell you how). They are subjective because they represent you personally, individually, and they do so from somewhat different perspectives. Each of these items has a distinctive function or purpose, too, and understanding that purpose can advantage you substantially.

In *The Virtual Advisor Online Companion* (http://www.thevirtual advisoronline.com), we address all of the objective and subjective components of the graduate application, and we take you from the earliest point of considering graduate study—exploring careers in psychology—to interviewing, and on to the final point of notifying programs about your decision to accept or decline their offers. In *The Pocket Companion*, we concentrate on those subjective components, the ones that are within your control and will make you stand out. It is those subjective components that most students worry about, too. You know what a good GPA looks like and what good GRE scores are (and we will tell you in *The Online Companion* what you need for different kinds of graduate programs), but most students are uncertain about the personal statement, vita, or letters of recommendation. Most students have never written a personal statement for graduate school, never drafted a vita for graduate study, and never even requested, much less read, any letters of recommendation for graduate schools.

But all that is about to change. Taken together, *The Virtual Advisor Online Companion* and *Pocket Companion* will give you a behind-the-scenes view of personal statements, vitas, and letters of recommendation and show you how to make yours shine. In fact, the whole purpose of *The Virtual Advisor* is to give you an insider's perspective on every facet of the graduate school application. By the time your application reaches the schools of your choice, you will have benefited from the considerable experience we bring to the table, experience that you can profit from *now*, instead of learning the hard way, after the fact.

And that is the purpose of *The Virtual Advisor.* It relieves you from having to say, "I only wish I knew *then* what I know *now.*" If you feel you would have been well served by having had a sneak peek at that job, that roommate, or that relationship well in advance of getting involved, then take heart. When it comes to your graduate applications, *The Virtual Advisor* gives you that glimpse and allows you to develop more informed, effective graduate application materials. In the end, our goal is to help you maximize your chances of getting into the top graduate schools of your choice. So let's get started!

Greg J. Neimeyer

Diane Stevenson

2

Developing Your Vita

In This Chapter You Will Learn:

❖ What a vita is and how it differs from a résumé

❖ How to begin, build, and organize a vita

❖ What to include and what to omit

❖ How to make sure nothing essential is missing

A curriculum vitae (hereafter *vita*) is the story of your academic life. As such, it represents your educational background and all related experience that qualifies you for graduate study. In that respect, a vita resembles a résumé, but because the "position" you are applying for is a spot in graduate school working with a certain professor, the emphasis is different. Writing a good vita involves starting early and keeping track of your activities so that you don't have to throw something together at the last minute—that's the ideal, at least. However, some students aren't sure if they plan on going to graduate school until perhaps the fall semester of their senior year in college, by which time—not to make you nervous—many opportunities have come and gone. But it's not too late, even if you've just now realized that you want to pursue an advanced degree. One of the first steps you need to take, in addition to preparing for the GRE in every spare moment you have, is putting together your application packet, for yourself and for your letter writers. Your vita is the first undertaking in that first step, because the personal statement draws heavily from it.

Before we get to the actual process involved in preparing the vita, let's take a moment to talk about this crucial document in more general terms. A vita is a neat, concise, error-free, comprehensive account of undergraduate experiences that prepare you for graduate school. It is a sales document. Your vita should be presented in an orderly and easily readable format that allows an admission committee member to scan it and extract the essentials in just a minute or two. Therefore, tight organization and a plain, clear format are essential, with order of importance a vital rule of thumb. Regarding appearance, your vita should be simple: plan on using heavy bond paper (white or off white) and a laser printer to create an attractive, easy-to-read document with 1-inch margins and white space to separate major category headings, which should be capitalized, underlined, or set off in boldface type. Some of those categories are mandatory—for example, name, complete contact information, including e-mail address and current and permanent telephone numbers (make sure your e-mail address and phone message are suitably professional), as well as educational background, including degrees. However, other category headings will vary according to your own personal experience and might include one or more of the following (listed in no particular order):

Professional Licenses and Certifications

Thesis

Conferences Attended

Teaching Experience

Technical Expertise

Honors and Awards

Research Experience

Grants

Volunteer/Clinical Experience

Publications

Computer Skills, Languages

Internships

Professional Memberships

Professional Presentations

Work Experience (Employment)

Study Abroad

Professional Service, Affiliations

Leadership

Committees

Community Involvement

Outreach

Counseling Experience

Clinical Experience

Related Professional Activities

References

❖ MAKING STRUCTURE OUT OF CHAOS

Your vita structures your experience. It organizes it. Without that structure and organization, your vita might meander from one thing to another, requiring the reader to make sense of your experience or to sort out the important features from the unimportant or irrelevant ones. But your vita will include ONLY relevant features, and ONLY important ones. YOU are going to be the one to decide what to include (and to exclude) and how to organize it. No two vitas are exactly alike, nor should they be. You are unique. Your experience is unique. And your vita should be unique, too.

The first rule of creating a vita is MOST IMPORTANT FIRST. If we examine for a moment the possible categories presented earlier, which would most immediately impress a reader looking for graduate school credentials? Of course, the answer to that question depends on the kind of program to which you are applying, but it is clear that study abroad is probably less important than research experience, and employment probably matters less than professional presentations. Therefore, when preparing your vita, remember that as readers glance through, they lose time, interest, and steam, so the initial context you create for yourself will carry forward to the end of the vita, where the lesser categories, such as professional memberships, are located. In this respect, writing a vita is similar to writing a newspaper story. Reporters start with a *lead*, which contains all of the critical information of interest, and from there they proceed to fill in the progressively less important details until the story is finished. Like a news story, your vita should resemble an upside-down triangle, with all of the most important information up top, tapering down toward the least significant features at the end. Although the particular experiences you choose to include in your vita are up to you, most vitas contain certain categories that are essential to applying for graduate school in psychology.

The most likely major categories in your vita will include the following, probably in this order: **Education** (including degree, date of anticipated graduation, GPA, relevant coursework, honors and awards, and information about your thesis, if you wrote one), **Research Experience** (including a description of what the laboratory investigates, the name of its principal investigator, and your position and responsibilities), **Volunteer/Clinical Experience** (including your position and responsibilities, the activity, and your dates of participation, along with location and the name of your supervisor), **Related Professional Activities** (including pursuits not mentioned earlier but relevant to graduate school), **Honors and Awards**, and **References** (not to be confused with letter of recommendation writers; see section titled "Framing Your Picture").

Let's take some time to talk about these various categories and, more importantly, how you generate the material that will help you develop them. In the following sections, we show you how to get from where you are now (at the starting line) to where you want to get (at the finish line) in relation to your vita.

❖ CONSTRUCTING YOUR VITA

One way to approach the creation of your vita is to start where you currently are: at a blank screen. Now try these simple steps:

1. First, brainstorm. Scribble. Jot down all activities, jobs, organizations, skills, experiences, strengths, honors and awards, special courses, volunteer work, licenses and certifications, test scores—everything you can think of that is potentially relevant to your graduate school interests. Consult family and friends, who may remember something you don't. Don't discount anything—an activity you might automatically

dismiss as trivial could end up being important. Give it a try. List your activities here.

_____
_____
_____
_____
_____
_____
_____
_____
_____

2. After you've committed everything to paper, you should have a mess, a long list of this-and-thats in no apparent order and of varying levels of importance. Now review the list and see if some logical categories emerge or if other experiences suggest themselves. Do you have more extracurricular sports listed than you remember being involved in? Did you forget those summers as a camp counselor? How about all the part-time jobs that helped pay for the trips to Europe (or tuition)? Brainstorming will help you not only recall events and activities that you wouldn't have otherwise considered but also see patterns emerging: the hard worker, the extraordinarily committed student volunteer, the mentor. In other words, distance yourself from the picture(s) taking shape so that you can do justice to the items in the list, and create a theme, at least in your own mind, for the purpose of writing the personal statement, which comes after the vita is finished. Approach your list as if it were an Impressionist painting, one that takes form as you step back to see images take shape from the particulars of the myriad individual points. Because you are the painter, you get to discern which images you see, so be creative! List possible themes or categories derived from your brainstorming:

_____
_____
_____
_____
_____

_____

_____

_____

_____

3. Once you have identified particular categories, some specific items or experiences that you have brainstormed may recede into the background because they weren't central to your composition, and others may drop out altogether because they aren't really part of the picture. Here's how it works. Suppose you came up with a list of experiences like this:

> Volunteer, Habitat for Humanity, spring vacations
>
> Camp counselor, summers
>
> Cashier, Bob's Burger Bites, part time
>
> Mentor, Big Brothers/Big Sisters, spring, two years
>
> Best Buddy Award, Youth Mentor Program
>
> Research assistant, Dr. Marlborough, cognitive psychology
>
> Research assistant, Dr. Smith, psychobiology, spring term, sophomore year
>
> Volunteer, Crisis Center, junior year
>
> Extramural volleyball team, spring semester, junior year
>
> Resident assistant, Bigler Hall, sophomore year
>
> Nanny, summers in high school
>
> Swim coach, The Little Fish team, freshman and sophomore years

This list might be used to create a picture of someone who enjoys working with children, based on the camp counselor experience plus the mentoring experience (and award), in addition to the nanny experience and the swim team coaching of small children (assuming the team is composed of children, given its name). If those entries are grouped together, then a **Related Experience** heading could be used. On the other hand, the writer might want to portray a vigorously physical person instead (as evidenced by extramural volleyball, swim coaching, and camp counselor experience), someone with great energy expended on simultaneous pursuits. If the counselor and coach experience are used to create that picture, then **Sports-Related Activities** might be an effective heading, particularly if the writer hopes to pursue sports psychology or wants to convey, for some reason, significant physical commitment and energy. Notice that *the same inventory might be used to paint very different pictures,* including a portrait of an altruistic person whose passion involves volunteer work (camp counseling, Habitat for Humanity, mentoring, crisis center), in which case the entries might be grouped under **Volunteer/Clinical Experience**. In a vita, there are no "right" or "wrong" categories per se, only categories that do a more or less effective job of conveying a goodness of fit between you and the programs to which you are applying.

❖ FRAMING YOUR PICTURE

Now that you're thinking about category headings, consider the format of the vita in general. Remember, you should have 1-inch margins flush left, as well as top and bottom, with the right margin set at 1 inch but unjustified. You should use only a 12-point font, leave a space between entries within a major category heading, and use caps, underlining, or boldface for emphasizing and organizing major categories (italics are hard to read, as is a font smaller than 12 points). Don't use different typefaces or font sizes, and avoid underlining for anything other than simple emphasis (the name of your position title, for example, and be sure to repeat this format if you use it even once). Do not splash your name across the top in a 64-point font (12 points in boldface caps is sufficient for emphasis).

Your name and current address should appear at the top, either centered or flush left, along with a phone number or a cell phone number and an e-mail address (avoid anything cute or offensive; *party girl@univ.edu* may be funny now, but it's not the image you want to conjure up for admissions committees). Your permanent address and phone number should be provided as well (nothing embarrassing on the answering machine, please), and now you've completed your essential contact information.

Drop a few spaces and begin your headings. As we describe in detail shortly, keep going until you've reached **References**, where you list three or four people, including their titles, university affiliations, and complete contact information. As you create your vita, keep in mind some important points:

- A vita can be any length! You do not have to squeeze everything onto one page. Most vitas are 2 to 3 pages; some are longer.
- Don't pad your vita with useless verbiage and exaggerated claims.

- Don't include your photograph, Social Security number, gender, political or religious affiliations, marital status, or career objective.
- Follow the same format within categories—for example, your position title (perhaps underlined or in bold), the name of the laboratory and its supervisor, the hours you worked per week, the inclusive dates of everything, and the location (your reader should not be expected to infer this information).
- Use the past tense for experiences that have ended and the present tense for current or ongoing participation.
- Do not use complete sentences; use fragments with action verbs like *recruited, managed, coordinated, acted as, supervised,* and so on.
- Use bullets to itemize important aspects of a category; use semicolons for less important aspects: *answered phones; recorded data; greeted participants.*

Your category headings are arranged in order of importance or relevance, with the most important first. So let's look at each of these categories individually. Because the point of a vita is to display your academic credentials, the first heading should therefore be **Education**, in all caps, flush left. Under that heading, list the university, the degree and discipline, and the anticipated date of graduation. List your GPA, any minors you might have, and the title of your thesis, if you did one. Also make sure you account for the rest of your academic life: if you earned an associate's degree at a community college, then it should be listed under **Education**, and so should relevant coursework, followed by a major category heading of **Honors and Awards**. The first vita entry, then, might look something like this:

EDUCATION

University of Cleveland, BA in Psychology, anticipated 2011

GPA in major: 3.70

GPA in minor (Sociology): 3.40

Overall GPA: 3.50

Thesis: "The Effect of Fad Dieting on Body Image Disorder," directed by Donald Smith, PhD

You may want to list selected coursework next (do not include grades), or you may want to provide a separate grouping of these courses under carefully crafted headings at the back of your vita instead (it's your vita, so you get to decide!). Your goal is to list only selected courses in areas of concentration relevant to your graduate school interests. Depending on your interests, your list might look like this:

> Relevant Coursework: Communicating Psychological Science, Abnormal Psychology, Eating Disorders, Advanced Cognitive Psychology, Personality Research Laboratory, Advanced Methods, Statistics II, Behavior Analysis

For most graduate programs **Research Experience** might be the next category, or possibly **Volunteer/Clinical Experience**, if you are seeking admission to applied master's degree programs in, for example, clinical, counseling, or school psychology. There is no prescription regarding particular headings or the particular order of those headings; everyone's experience is different, and graduate programs differ as well. However, your goal is to portray yourself in the strongest possible light in relation to the programs to which you are applying. The vita is a sales pitch, so create your category headings and orderings accordingly.

If research experience is important to your graduate school plans, and for that reason is next up on your vita, then you have to consider what counts as research experience. In short, membership in a laboratory qualifies you as having research experience; membership in a course that has an accompanying laboratory component does not. Research experiences include any research-related activities in which you engage other than ordinary courses, such as research methods, statistics, and so forth. Most universities offer different levels of research involvement. "Introduction to Research," "Individual Work," and "Senior Thesis" are examples of individual research experiences of progressively greater responsibility; these courses are highly individualized and often available on a variable-credit basis. Few universities actually require these courses, but most offer them; they are self-inflicted—that is, elective or optional—and are designed precisely to allow students the opportunity of gaining research skills, experience, and focus. For that reason, all of these courses and experiences are noteworthy. They speak to your interest in research and your initiative in pursuing professional development above and beyond the call of duty, qualities that strengthen your prospects as a graduate student, where a premium is placed on just such features. For these research experience entries, remember to use reverse chronological order—that is, the most recent experience would be listed first, followed by the next most recent, and so on into the past. Be consistent in your presentation, always start with your position title, and be complete (but don't pad) in your description of duties and responsibilities. Such a category might look like this:

RESEARCH EXPERIENCE

Senior Undergraduate Research Assistant, July 2007–May 2008

Dr. Robert Roberts, Developmental Laboratory, Psychology Department, UCMF.

Laboratory investigates how participants aged 18–65 use knowledge to cope with daily stressors. Duties included administering baseline testing; conducting phone interviews; entering data using SPSS; scanning image data using XFileSupreme; and transcribing taped interviews using the coding protocol Xanadu.

Research Assistant, January 2007–July 2007

Dr. Bertha Bornwright, Personality Laboratory, Psychology Department, UCMF.

Laboratory investigates how moral and ethical psychology manifests in crisis situations. Duties included conducting literature reviews; contributing to questionnaires used in study; supervising undergraduate coders; reporting results in a weekly meeting with Principal Investigator; updating databases using INFAX.

Research Assistant, April 2006–January 2007

Dr. Mary Lamb, Child Trauma Laboratory, Psychology Department, UCMF.

Laboratory investigates effects of one-time trauma on children in foster care. Duties included coding taped interviews using Xanadu; recruiting participants through state databases; organizing laboratory materials.

Publications follow from **Research Experience,** so this is a natural category to come next. Not too many undergraduates publish, although they might be credited in a publication or be part of one or more paper presentations. If so, great! You can always create a category called **Publications and Professional Presentations** and include all of those accomplishments there. Don't forget your senior thesis, too, which might be listed as an unpublished manuscript if it has not yet been submitted for review and possible publication. Follow American Psychological Association guidelines for correctly citing papers and presentations, and don't forget that even one publication or presentation is stellar, so be sure to include it, even if there are no others in that category. If you have such a category, it might look like this:

PUBLICATIONS AND PRESENTATIONS

Smith, S.V., & Dalkin, D. (2009, March). *The effects of alcohol use on prosocial behavior in college students*. Paper presented at the annual meeting of the Midwestern Psychological Association, Columbus, OH.

Dalkin, D. (2009). *Alcohol-induced disinhibition among college students: An exploratory study*. Manuscript in preparation, University of St. Cloud.

After **Research Experience** and **Publications and Professional Presentations**, an important category might include **Volunteer Work**. Remember the distinction between *volunteering* and *working*, however: you do not get paid to be a volunteer, whereas you do get paid for work. Sometimes, students will begin by volunteering, and subsequently work at the same agency as a paid employee. Those two experiences would be listed separately, but beware of listing the same activity in two places. In the example of volunteer-to-work, however, your change of position would be reflected by your title, as well as by the dates. Also remember that instead of distinguishing between paid and volunteer experience it might be beneficial to have a larger, more inclusive group under a heading such as **Clinical Experience**. Such a category might include volunteer and paid experiences, and it might look like this:

CLINICAL EXPERIENCE

<u>Crisis Counselor</u>, The Neighborhood Safe Place, 67 Bay Shore Drive, Miami, Florida 42956. May 2007–September 2007, volunteered 20 hours/week. Supervisor: Alan Shore, 123-456-7890.

- Answered hotline during the midnight-to-dawn shift; referred callers to local specialized agencies
- Supervised required training of new volunteers in suicide prevention strategies

---

(Continued)

(Continued)

> Peer Counselor, XYZ Fraternity, University of Mars, 123 Lunar Way, Galaxy, Florida 45012. September 2006–May 2007, volunteered approximately 10 hours/week. Duties included meeting one-on-one with fraternity members experiencing problems, most often with substance abuse, homesickness, and relationship difficulties.
>
> Baby Cuddler, University Hospital, 111 College Avenue, Galaxy, Florida, 45012. September 2006–May 2007, volunteered 10 hours/week. Supervisor: Martha Washington. Comforted, rocked, and sang to infants in neonatal intensive care unit.
>
> Camp Counselor, In Vivo Camp for Transitional Youth, 666 Rock Bottom Avenue, Torrid, Florida 45012. May 2006–August 2006. Full-time paid position. Supervisor: Dr. Harley Davidson, 231-476-9078. Duties included recording daily behaviors of six campers, aged 12–14, using Lorax coding system; preparing and serving individualized meals; directing evening activities; monitoring sleep patterns.
>
> Construction Director, Habitat for Humanity, local University of Mars branch: outreach to communities in Virginia, South Carolina, and Georgia. Spring vacations, 2003–2006. Paid position. Supervisor: Barbara Jones, 365-965-9423. Duties included training 4–9 volunteers in principles and rudimentary practices of rehabbing dwellings. Oversaw progress and reported milestones to supervisor.

After the categories of **Education, Research,** and **Clinical** (or **Volunteer) Experience**, a catchall category is often useful. This catchall category can contain important and relevant information that simply doesn't fit neatly into the other categories. Consider the following as an example. Imagine that, after you list your education, research, and clinical experience, you still have the following items scribbled on your brainstorming list:

Treasurer, Alpha Gamma Beta fraternity, junior year

Member, Friends of the Library, junior year

Vice president, Suicide Prevention Club, sophomore year

Phone hotline counseling trainer, Crisis Center, junior year

Supervisor, Crisis Center volunteers, senior year

President, Campus Friends of Animals, junior year

Member, Campus Animal Shelter Volunteer, sophomore and junior years

These seven random listings cover a three-year period. Despite their diversity, however, patterns can be extracted from them. Step back and you might see some potential themes emerge. Helping animals and people (reflecting a humanitarian concern for the welfare of others) might be one. Another might be leadership, given the offices held: treasurer, vice president, and president. Ideally, you would take note of these trends and make the most of them by creating a heading such as **Leadership**, under which entries for the crisis center (first a trainer, then a supervisor) might be listed, as well as various organizational offices or positions. Leadership is always a good category, and it can be an effective catchall for collecting and reflecting experience that may not easily fit elsewhere but nonetheless might well be important to graduate programs looking to admit future leaders in their fields.

In fact, we have a good story about leadership and the tendency of students sometimes to throw away really worthwhile entries just because they don't apply directly to psychology. One semester, a student was brainstorming and drafting her vita and personal statement; it looked a bit skimpy, and she was worried about her lack of research experience. This student looked tired in class and was having trouble meeting with her research partner because of multiple other obligations, but not much was listed on her vita. After a bit of prompting, she revealed that she was an officer in one organization, an officer in another organization, sat on the board of directors of the student union, and was organizing various events for yet another organization to which she belonged. All told, she had previously either held office in or headed up committees in about 15 clubs, sororities, and organizations, and she was currently actively involved in several others, yet this student had listed none of these on her vita because they were not "in psychology"! Finally she did list them, and she was nominated by a professor for one of her university's student leadership awards, which included dinner at the university president's house. By the time she graduated, this student had won the top award for service that her university had to offer. It goes without saying that her revised personal statement included mention of her deep commitment to the ideal of service; her ultimate career plans, which would require great vision and time to achieve, became very plausible in the context of her limitless energy and leadership experience. The moral of this story is this: in your scribblings and brainstorming, include everything! You don't always know what might be important or valuable when you step back to take a look at it from another perspective.

After **Leadership** (or some other catchall category), you may want to note **Honors and Awards** (although some people prefer to list academic honors and awards under the heading **Education**). Here you can think broadly about honors and awards. Maybe you have officially been recognized by a club, organization, department, or university for your outstanding research, leadership, or service. If so, great! But if not, keep thinking. Students often skip this potential category simply because they don't consider themselves as having been singled out for recognition when in fact they have been. Have you ever made the dean's list or the president's honor roll for your GPA? Are you on a scholarship or fellowship of some sort? Have you been awarded an Honors or High Honors designation for your GPA, your senior thesis, or both? Are you a member of Psi Chi or Phi Beta Kappa? Have you been selected or inducted into any honor organizations on the basis of your achievement or accomplishments? All of these things count as honors and awards, and you should include them to underscore the fact that you have been recognized for your accomplishments.

Once you start thinking about honors and awards, you may realize that some entries might fit into other categories, such as **Memberships**, and that's fine. The rule of thumb is that a category should have at least two entries and, if there are a sufficient number of entries of a different kind within a given group, it might be broken out into a second group. Being elected president of Psi Chi might go under **Leadership** if it is joined by at least one other similar experience; if not, it might go under **Memberships**, **Honors and Awards**, or **Related Experience**.

References can make a valuable final category. Not to be confused with letters of recommendation, the term *references* refers to individuals who are willing to stand in support of your application to graduate study but are not necessarily writing a letter for you. Letter writers usually are people who know you well, often across a sustained period of time, a range of different contexts, or both. They are well situated to comment on you and your qualifications, and they can do so from the perspective of being faculty members who understand the nature of graduate study. References, by contrast, may include individuals who know you only in more circumscribed settings (e.g., your supervisor at a place you volunteered for a semester, the coordinator of Habitat for Humanity with whom who you worked). These people know you in contexts that would allow them to comment on certain qualities, such as your maturity, dedication, ability to work well with others, and so on, but not necessarily on your skills or aptitudes in relation to your chosen area of graduate study. To include someone as a reference, you have to ask permission ("May I use you as a reference in case graduate schools wanted to ask about me and your experience of working with me?"). References often do not actually get contacted, but they serve an important function nonetheless. They advertise, at an implicit level, that you have a whole network of professionals who are willing to stand behind you. They tell the admissions committee, "Look at all of the people who think highly of this applicant—she (or he) must be terrific!"

When you list references, put the person's name and title first, followed by his or her contact information. A sample **Reference** category might look like this:

REFERENCES

Tom Stoddard, PhD, Director of Seneca County Volunteer Center, 2222 Talcon Avenue, St. Petersburg, Florida 45012. Phone: 333-123-4567. E-mail: tstoddard@volunteer.org

Christine Dia, Coordinator, Eckard Youth Camps, 1776 Castillo de San Marcos Avenue, St. Augustine, Florida 45012. Phone: 212-289-5890. E-mail: cdia@eckard.com

---

Now let's put all these pieces together and take a look at a sample vita for an imaginary applicant who is applying for doctoral programs in child clinical psychology.

SALLY MARSTON

Permanent address:	Sigma Xu Sorority
1213 Hope Way	6502 Sorority Way
Halifax, West Virginia 12365	Anchorage, Alaska 03976
327-365-9123	sm@scyu.edu
	cell: 365-976-2634

EDUCATION

University of Alaska, BA in Psychology, anticipated June 2011, with honors

Minor: Education

Overall GPA: 3.65

GPA in major: 3.80

GPA in minor: 3.50

(Continued)

(Continued)

Relevant Coursework: Children and Families, Child Psychology, Educating At-Risk Children, Family Counseling, Personality Theory and Parental Practices, Family Dynamics, The New American Family Structure

RESEARCH EXPERIENCE

Senior Honors Thesis: Developed and defended "Attention-Deficit Disorder in College Students." Conceptualized the study, ran participants, wrote the thesis, and defended it before a faculty committee. Supervisor: Dr. Sherlock Watson.

Research Assistant, Developmental Psychology Laboratory, Dr. Homer Hampton. August 2010–May 2011. Duties included assisting with the data collection in two studies of children with impulse control disorder (ages 7–10). Conducted interviews, behavioral observations, and codings.

PRESENTATIONS AND PUBLICATIONS

Marston, S., & Watson, S. (2009). *Attention-deficit disorder in college students.* Manuscript in preparation.

Watson, S., Marston, S., & Stevenson, D. (2008, March). *Impulsive behavior in late adolescence.* Paper presented at the annual meeting of the Southeastern Psychological Association, Atlanta, GA.

CLINICAL EXPERIENCE

Crisis Counselor, Hotline USA, 49 College Way, Anchorage, Alaska 39567. Supervisor: Mary Howland (968-078-4598). Volunteer, 20 hours/week. September 2008–present. Answer hotline calls for those in crisis. Primarily weekend and holiday shifts. Train new volunteers.

Comforter, Children's Home Shelter, Anchorage, Alaska. Current part-time employee for organization housing battered children. No address or contact information allowable. Duties include informally listening and talking to sexually and physically abused children admitted for temporary stays prior to placement in foster homes. Ages range from 2 to 14 years; children most often admitted directly from hospital.

Counselor in Training, Home Alternatives, 579 Norman Highway, Daytona, Florida 40239. May–September 2008, full-time volunteer. Supervisor: Dr. Howard Hughes (345-069-2587). Assisted director in all aspects of family counseling:

- Attended counseling sessions and provided secondary voice
- Met with children individually, recorded their narratives

- Conferred with director after sessions to suggest treatment options
- Researched current alternative family therapies and reported them to director
- Trained new volunteers on practices and procedures

INTERNSHIP

<u>Child Advocacy Center</u>, 2067 County Road, Richmond, Virginia 23221. May–September 2007. Awarded full-time residency status and full tuition to nationally recognized program for future family counselors. Attended intensive training modules in the following areas:

- Recognizing signs of distress in children under age 5
- Researching best practices techniques for families experiencing financial hardships
- Understanding dynamics leading to child abandonment
- Applying current research to obtain best results in foster care placement

RELATED EXPERIENCE

<u>Mentor</u>, Big Brothers/Big Sisters, 56 Orange Blossom Way, Anchorage, Alaska 39567. Supervisor: John Smith (390-049-8456). January 2007–present. Three hours/week, with breaks for summers and holidays.

<u>Tutor</u>, Adams Elementary School, 30 Orange Blossom Way, Anchorage, Alaska 39567. Supervisor: Cathy Smith. September 2008–present. Provide after-school help with reading and study skills for third graders, two days/week.

PROFESSIONAL SERVICE/LEADERSHIP

<u>President</u>, Child Advocates, Campus Branch, University of Alaska. October 2008–present. Organization helps local agencies raise money and meet emergency staffing needs at organizations in three-county area. Duties include chairing monthly meetings; evaluating requests for assistance from local agencies; and serving as contact person for Angel of Mercy Hospital.

<u>Treasurer</u>, Child Advocates, Campus Branch, University of Alaska. October 2006–2007. Managed budget for organization and allocated funds for assistance to local agencies.

HONORS AND AWARDS

National Merit Finalist
President's Honor Roll, sophomore–senior years
Dean's Honor Roll, freshman year
Outstanding Undergraduate Poster Presentation, Department of Psychology, University of Alaska, Spring 2009

(Continued)

(Continued)

> **SPECIAL SKILLS**
>
> Fluent in Spanish, French, and American Sign Language
>
> Proficient in Memory Lab software, XFileSupreme, and Xanadu coding system
>
> **REFERENCES**
>
> Dr. Howard Hughes, Home Alternatives
> 579 Norman Highway
> Daytona, Florida 40239
>
> Dr. Jill Jones, Psychology Department
> University of Alaska
> 123 Cold Road
> Anchorage, Alaska 39567
>
> Dr. Sam Rigor, Psychology Department
> University of Alaska
> 123 Cold Road
> Anchorage, Alaska 39567
>
> Dr. Lola Allbright, Psychology Department
> University of Alaska
> 123 Cold Road
> Anchorage, Alaska 39567

Before we listen to advice from current graduate students, let's highlight a few important points:

- A vita is highly individualized; there is no formula for creating the perfect vita.
- Information you consider irrelevant may end up being important, so list *everything* in your brainstorming.
- Pay attention to detail! A crowded, sloppy vita says something about you, just as a clearly arranged, tidy, carefully constructed one does.
- Establish your format and stick to it, using consistent underlining, boldface, and so on.
- Don't use complete sentences, and don't exaggerate your role—but don't be so modest that your entries lack complete information.
- Create several drafts so that you (and your closest friends or mentors) can compare.
- Add experiences as you go along and seek out new ones NOW if you find yourself lacking.

FEATURE

Q & A: The Vita

Q: What's the difference between a vita and a résumé?

A: A résumé is used for job searches, is often limited to one page, and includes an occupational objective (e.g., "to become a sales manager"). A vita reflects the relevant educational and professional experience needed for graduate school, can be any length, and does not contain a job objective.

Q: How long should my vita be?

A: As long as it needs to be! There is no page limit, but there are some constraining features to consider. Time is one. Vitas are reviewed for only a few minutes, so make sure your important information comes first and is emphasized by being clearly presented.

Q: What counts as padding in a vita?

A: Books you've read, favorite pastimes, travel, and pets would be good examples of padding. But sometimes the line is blurry. Travel, for example, might be an essential category if you are interested in multicultural counseling, but listing a cruise wouldn't be a good idea.

Q: My vita seems to be the outline for my personal statement. Is that OK?

A: Yes, it's fine. These two documents are companion pieces, with the vita representing the sum total of your qualifications for graduate school and the personal statement telling the story derived from those single-line entries. The vita might be used before or during the interview, whereas the personal statement wouldn't be, so redundancy isn't an issue.

Q: I'm a member of some clubs and organizations that have nothing to do with psychology. Should I include them?

A: Probably. The balance would tip in favor of their inclusion if you find meaningful ways to group these activities. Your memberships might convey a sense of you as an involved individual with a range of interests. However, be advised not to list a Star Trek club or anything potentially offensive. Avoid listing religious or political organizations unless they truly define you and you have many, many entries over time.

Q: What about work experience?

A: Absolutely, along with the complete contact information of your employers if possible. Flipping burgers, babysitting, lifeguarding—all of these jobs speak to your work ethic and ability to manage time.

FEATURE

Words of Wisdom From Successful Graduate Applicants

1. Keep your [vita] neat and organized. Align all bullets. Have the same number of indentations. Arrange topics by importance. Do not drown your [vita] with paragraphs or long lists. If your reader wants to see more, that information can be requested. —Kisha R.

2. First, look at examples. Oftentimes, professors post their vitas online. Look at several and then find one that suits you. Once you have completed yours, have as many people critique it as possible, especially your professors. Admissions committees will be looking at potentially hundreds of applications, so an ill-conceived vita can be deleterious to the overall impression of your application. In addition, your accomplishments may be overlooked because your vita was not well organized. You did a lot to prepare yourself for this graduate application process. Get credit for it. —Lance D.

3. I think it is beneficial when the vita is coherent and illustrates an area of particular interest. The vita should convey that you have set your mind on a goal and have participated in relevant activities that prepare you to achieve this goal. In my opinion, vitas that jump all over the place may suggest that the candidate is indecisive about the path he or she is pursuing. —Peter T.

4. Your vita should be well organized and easy to read. The admissions committee may receive hundreds of vitas, so your [vita] needs to get your important qualities, experience, and education across effectively and efficiently. I organized my [vita] with my contact information at the top; education directly following; and continued with awards and honors, poster presentations, research experience (with the supervisor listed first, followed by the research purpose, and bullets of my roles on each team), teaching experience (formatted similarly to research experience), technology/research skills, extracurricular activities, and finally references. —Rene M.

5. Make your vita concise, but don't forget important details. You may not realize an asset you have. —Taryn B.

6. Don't pad it. For some part-time jobs, it's fine if your résumé is a glowing, wonderful festival of beautiful lies. This is not a good idea for grad school applications, though. If you claim expertise in some statistical method, for example, be prepared to defend your knowledge of that topic (one prof at an interview called my knowledge of SEM and the justification for my first authorship on my senior thesis, but I was able to satisfactorily prove that those things were true). —Giselle M.

7. Tell the story of your life (vita), but also the story of your match with the kind of program you're applying to. —Terri H.

8. Look at other vitas and ask for a lot of feedback. —Larry O.

3

Crafting Your Personal Statement

In This Chapter You Will Learn:

- ❖ The vital importance of prewriting (brainstorming) as well as the three most important techniques of editing for style
- ❖ The value of self-examination
- ❖ The trick to strong organization
- ❖ The single most important thing you can do to increase your chance of acceptance

Prepare for a painful experience, but don't delay. Writing the personal statement is like taking the GREs—those who procrastinate because the task is distasteful don't do as well as those willing to forge ahead, put in the time, and get the job done. Remember: your vita, personal statement, transcripts, letters of recommendation, and GREs all combine to create a total package, so what might be lacking in one area can be somewhat compensated for in another. Of course, the personal statement is the only part of your application that presents you as *you*, so it's distinctive; everything else reflects either what you have done (e.g., your transcripts, your vita) or what someone else has to say about you (your letters of recommendation). The unique purpose of the personal statement, as a companion piece to the vita, is to convey your style, attitude, values, and writing ability. So expect to draft many, many versions to meet this challenge.

❖ APPROACHING THE TASK: GENERAL COMMENTS

It's not easy to communicate the essence of you, so let's talk about how you can approach this task. First, download the application forms from the schools you have researched and to which you are going to apply. Then read the directions regarding their personal statements, specifically the guidelines concerning content and length. Some schools have a particular question you must answer in about 500 words. If that is the case, refer to that question repeatedly as you write: treat the exercise like a take-home test. If you are applying to, say, six schools (and you know exactly why you've chosen each because you've listened to *The Online Advisor*), and each one has a specific question you must address, then you must write six different personal statements. Your personal statement *must* be tailored to each school, because you are arguing, in essence, that you and the graduate program are a good fit, an excellent match. How would you build a case for that very important point unless you knew the program thoroughly? In fact, to start building your list of possible schools (and just for practice), how about listing your top four here (along with their instructions for writing the personal statement):

1.
_____
_____
_____
_____
_____

2.

_____
_____
_____
_____
_____

3.

_____
_____
_____
_____
_____

4.

_____
_____
_____
_____
_____

Perhaps you found similarities among the different instructions for writing the personal statement, because most schools are interested in knowing some version of the following:

- Why are you applying to this school?
- What makes you a strong candidate?
- What made you choose this particular field and stick with it?
- What experiences have you had that cut you from the pack?

The two most important bits of advice to begin with involve steps you probably would most like to avoid; however, if you want to write a splendid personal statement, heed these recommendations for the *before* and the *after*.

❖ THE BEFORE: RESEARCH!

Every school has ample information online about its areas of research, its overall acceptance rate, the faculty involved in particular areas of research and the number of graduate students they have, as well as the GRE scores required for acceptance, along with GPA cutoffs and other facts you need to know. Some schools will post very general numbers in that regard—they stipulate that your GPA, for example, should be a 3.00 or above, but actually a 3.5 is closer to the mark. Remember, you intend to spend the next several years of your life at this place, so choose carefully, to the best of your knowledge. The point is this: study the schools to which you are applying. There is simply no substitute for this legwork. If you want to become a professional in this field, now is the time to start.

Once you know, on the basis of your research, which faculty member you think you might like to work with, find that person's vita online; it's generally available through the institution's Web site. Read up on that professor's research interests, and look at his or her publications. By the titles alone, can you tell whether the professor is currently conducting research in an area that interests you? Did the person formerly publish in an area that interests you? Take the time to read some of the articles listed on the vita. Then ask yourself the following questions:

- Is this faculty member going in a direction I want to take?
- How can I find out if this faculty member is accepting new graduate students?
- Is this faculty member likely to view my experience and interests as a good fit with the direction he or she is taking? Am I capable of contributing to this person's research?

The next step, of course, in addition to answering the preceding questions, is listing faculty members at the four schools to which you plan to apply, along with their interests and the titles of recent publications:

1.
_____
_____
_____
_____

2.

_____
_____
_____
_____
_____

3.

_____
_____
_____
_____
_____

4.

_____
_____
_____
_____
_____

Now that you have read some articles and done further research on the professor, e-mail that person asking a question, or commenting on a specific article or on his or her research. You might ask about articles in press but not yet published (it takes about two years from the time a project is completed to the time it appears in a journal). If the faculty member responds to you, reply with an e-mail expressing appreciation and continued interest. At this point, you have done what may be the single most important thing to enhance your chances of getting into graduate school in psychology: you have established a relationship. Importantly, this relationship is based on shared interests (the faculty member's research), and this meeting point is of great interest to admissions committees. But be sure that whatever interests you express are sincere ones.

Here's a true story. An undergraduate interested in a particular graduate program e-mailed the professor he thought he'd like to work with, remarking on her research and commenting that he intended to apply to the program. She immediately e-mailed back, saying she would keep an eye out for his application and asked if he would be interested in working on so-and-so. With great excitement, he responded by saying "Yes, indeed," thinking that her question was conversational and fairly wide ranging. It turned out that it wasn't. To make a long story short, he was accepted into the program; during the first week of graduate school he met with his dissertation advising committee about *the very question she had asked him*, much to his surprise. It turns out that the friendly professor considered his reply to be an affirmative regarding a dissertation topic! Clearly, this student didn't realize when he eagerly e-mailed back that he had committed himself to a certain line of research. As things turned out, he was able to change that topic a bit, and all ended well, but note that once you e-mail a professor, he or she takes your interest seriously.

❖ THE AFTER: EDIT! REVISE! REWRITE! RECONSIDER! START OVER! WRITE A SECOND DRAFT!

Remember, the personal statement is a companion piece to the vita. Imagine you have conducted an experiment and you're writing up the results; then imagine you have to create a discussion section making sense of those results. What do they mean? How can they be interpreted? Your vita is the experiment, and your personal statement is the discussion. Your vita outlines, in the briefest, most concise form, your accomplishments and activities. Your personal statement draws conclusions from that concise representation. So you worked in a laboratory—so what? The personal statement answers that question.

The vita includes facts, but the personal statement brings those facts together to create a picture of a highly motivated and ambitious student ready to take on graduate work. Or perhaps it crafts a picture of a curious, inquisitive student with an unquenchable desire to contribute to the field. Or perhaps it paints a picture of a student who has overcome great obstacles and is well prepared to withstand the rigors of graduate work—do you get the picture? Your vita could be the foundation for perhaps 10 different personal statements, all of which would be true, but by emphasizing different details, drawing different conclusions, beginning with an anecdote instead of hard-hitting information, or using certain words instead of others, a different version of you comes across. Therefore, in the personal statement, don't just repeat information contained in the vita—USE that information to fashion a person. What have you learned from the experiences listed on your vita? What skills do you find most valuable? What insights have you gained? How has your academic background prepared you to tackle the challenges of graduate school? Once you realize how creative this process is, you might actually find yourself enjoying it!

Remember also that the personal statement should be persuasive, with an underlying argument that implies in almost every sentence why you should be chosen over another, equally qualified applicant. There is little point in saying you want to help people—who doesn't? If you are applying to a professional program (e.g., clinical, counseling, school psychology), then the admissions committee will assume that fact anyway, and your letters of recommendation will surely speak to your interest in the welfare of others.

In this section, we address many questions students typically have about writing the personal statement, but we do so with the understanding that you will also do the following:

- Research *personal statement* online to get as much advice as possible
- Consult family and friends (as well as professors and peers) who can refresh your memory or tell you things about yourself
- Read your first draft aloud so that you hear clunkers (listening differs from reading)
- Have your personal statement read back to you so that you can hear your own words said by someone else
- Revise, and revise again—many times

In other words, neither we nor any other source should be the one and only you consult. Only you can make the final decision about what to include in the vita and personal statement, and which professors to ask for letters of recommendation. Ultimately, these decisions are up to you, but getting as much input and feedback as possible before, during, and after will enable you to make the best choices you can, so step up and start this agonizing process, because the minute you begin, you start heading toward the finish line!

❖ WHY IS WRITING A PERSONAL STATEMENT SUCH AN UNPLEASANT EXPERIENCE? GETTING STARTED

Writing, in general, is not an activity most people eagerly pursue, because translating thoughts into words on paper to create a formal text is difficult. Who joyfully undertakes writing a 20-page paper or a letter to Uncle Rupert? Making sure words represent your thoughts (and your thoughts represent you) takes a mighty effort. Returning to a draft to make the language more precise, to change an example, to combine sentences for fluency, to correct grammar, is exceedingly difficult. In fact, most people think one draft is enough—having to revisit your own prose and understand how it can be improved seems too much to ask! But on this one occasion, it's vital. So break the task into steps. The first step is *pre*-prewriting:

1. Read sample personal statements online. There are lots of them, everywhere. Some are good, some aren't. At this point, become the critic you need to be. Remember, only you can decide the approach to take. Reading lots of personal statements takes the sting out of the task you confront—it's just a matter of immersing yourself in the subject, the job that awaits you. Once you get a feel for what personal statements sound like, you will be better able to start your draft. Now take a moment to jot some notes to yourself about the personal statements you liked and those you didn't:

_____

_____

_____

_____

_____

2. Read advice about writing personal statements. There is lots of it, everywhere—in books, online. Some is good, some isn't. Some will apply to you, some won't. Some tips for writing personal statements in other disciplines, such as law, might give you certain insights, but again, you have to familiarize yourself with this subject, just as you would any other subject in a class or elsewhere. Become an expert; understand why some tips are NOT for you and in what ways you can make use of the tips that are. What advice do you plan on following, and what pitfalls do you want to avoid? Give *yourself* some good advice:

_____

_____

_____

_____

3. Know your word limit. Most schools will give one. If not, plan on writing about 500 words, or two typed pages.

Only after you have perused the information available to you online should you begin the second step, *prewriting*, also known as *brainstorming*, *scribbling*, "jotting down ideas," *clustering*, and so forth. This step calls for stopping to think about your life. So before you become tense over diction, try to remember everything you've ever done—every camp counseling position you've ever had, every babysitting job. Also, consult your vita, because you've undertaken this scribbling process once, so accessing the information already generated is a great idea. But a prewriting personal statement scribble might also help you think of a hook, a way into the story you have to tell about yourself.

We have many happy endings to recount about students who met with great success, but consider this one: a student started a class at the beginning of her junior year with only nanny experience. That's it—no laboratories, no teaching assistantships under her belt, no volunteer experience. Although she planned on going to graduate school, her vita was less than skimpy—it took up about one half of a page. She had cared for one autistic child, but because of her time with this boy, she knew she wanted to pursue behavior therapy. Her personal statement recounted some incidents with the child, but the statement was short and seriously lacking. Fortunately, this student faced her shortcomings before it was too late. One important point is this: no matter where you are in your undergraduate studies, sometimes just getting under way with this process allows you to fill in the blanks, so to speak.

The student in our vignette did just that. She took the bull by the horns and at the end of the semester, after coming a great, great distance already, asked one of us if she could be a teaching assistant the next semester. She also become an active member of research laboratories and enrolled in a graduate course, and she was finally admitted into graduate study at one of the premier institutions that does the work in which she was interested. Because this student started thinking about graduate school early, because she encountered herself on the page, sized up the situation, and had a reckoning, she was able to hustle herself into position to add impressive credentials to her vita. Her personal statement used the same nanny experience as the jumping-off point, but instead of being the focus of the statement, it became the springboard for the other experiences she accrued after realizing her shortfalls.

Pause for a moment and think about the following; then list whatever you can remember that applies using the blanks provided:

1. Important events in your life (your uncle's illness, your accident, a conversation you had with a parent, finding a bag of money, being bitten by a dog, etc.)

_____
_____
_____
_____
_____

2. Important influences in your life (teachers, parents, friends, courses, sayings)

_____
_____
_____
_____
_____

3. Books you've read (*Sybil*), movies you've seen (*A Beautiful Mind*)

_____
_____
_____
_____
_____

4. Vacations you've taken, family moves you've made

_____
_____
_____
_____

5. Special talents or skills (e.g., you speak three languages)

_____
_____
_____
_____

6. Examples set by siblings, parents, and friends (positive *or* negative)

_____
_____
_____
_____

7. People you admire and want to emulate (or vice versa)

_____
_____
_____
_____

8. Life lessons you've learned (a lesson might be based on anything)

_____
_____
_____
_____

9. Hardships you've faced, obstacles you've overcome (e.g., failure, pain, poverty, illness)

_____

_____

_____

_____

_____

10. Favorite sayings or anecdotes

_____

_____

_____

_____

_____

11. Memories (good or bad)

_____

_____

_____

_____

_____

12. Crises (this category might be subsumed under Item No. 9)

_____

_____

_____

_____

_____

13. Insights and turning points (e.g., often, students begin their undergraduate careers convinced they want to become doctors; after a few chemistry and physics courses, however, they change their minds)

_____

_____

14. Your parents' hopes and wishes for you, family traditions (and your adherence, or lack thereof, to them)

_____

_____

_____

_____

_____

15. Problems and issues (an ongoing estrangement with a friend that was resolved, a family feud that interrupted your life)

_____

_____

_____

_____

_____

You need to search for details that set you apart from everyone else who is applying—and from the list you've just generated, you should discover something to extract that ONLY YOU can say! Your scribbled prewriting for the personal statement might look like this:

"Brevity is the soul of wit"—love of reading

Margie's suicide—effect on her brother

Getting rid of the dog in the 3rd grade

Uncle Ben's favorite saying

A Boy Called "It"

Biology and psychology courses in high school

Adopt-a-Road cleanup project

My first AP class—fascinated with psychology

Learning lab techniques in Dr. Fenker's cognitive lab

Breaking a test tube—lab quarantine

Worrying about my GPA—honors?

Joining Psi Chi

My friendship with Bob

Participating in the Bystander Effect experiment

Learning difference between experiment and correlation

Summer spent watching psychologically based movies

Learning SPSS

Doing the class presentation in my social psychology class

Serving as peer counselor

Large class vs. small class

My visit to Washington, DC (Georgetown)

Talks with Graduate Coordinator

Seminar on applying to graduate school!!

Letters: Dr. Smith, Dr. Jones, and ?

So give it a try. Take a few minutes and jot down everything that you can think of that has represented important or distinctive experiences for you. Don't worry—you don't need to work them all into your personal statement. You are just looking for an angle that is distinctly you.

You might also try listing your unique traits and characteristics, either ones you think you have or ones that others (to whom you've spoken for the purpose of making this list) claim to find true about you. In this scribble, you should consider WHY you are applying to graduate school and what characteristics, specifically, would contribute to your success. Ask yourself (and others, as applicable) the following questions:

1. What is my greatest strength as a student, or investigator? How does that strength make me a good candidate for graduate school?

2. Why do I want to go to graduate school? Why do I believe I *need* to go to graduate school? (Your goals might be better accomplished via another route.)

3. What are my ultimate goals? What do I see myself doing 10 years from now? (Be sure you can distinguish between a *goal* and a *dream*. A goal is realistic, has short-term milestones that need to be met, and is obtainable, whereas a dream is a vague desire, such as "I want to be rich.")

4. How hard have I worked, and at doing what? Specifically, what is my work experience? All work experience, as we pointed out in chapter 2, counts, but when you answer this question think about what kind of worker you are: a hard and diligent worker, a worker who needs to make money to pay for school, a creative and imaginative worker, a joyful worker. Your attitude toward work says a lot about you. Also, what have you learned about yourself by working hard toward a goal? Have you narrowed your research interests? Developed great leadership skills? Gained independence?

5. Why did I choose the specific area of psychology I now want to pursue, and when did I choose it? Remember: do not list "I want to help people" as a reason for going into counseling psychology, or "I want to understand more about how the brain works" as a reason for applying to programs in behavioral neuroscience. Do not allow yourself to use generalities.

6. Specifically, what fascinates and compels me? What do I want to know more about?

7. How do I think I might contribute to the field or profession?

8. What is important to me? Having a career? Making money? Becoming famous? Conducting research?

9. Do I dislike anything in particular—children, older people, violent people?

10. Finally, why should this program accept *me*, rather than someone else just as qualified?

Your second scribbled prewriting for the personal statement might look like this:

Imaginative, creative, independent, great ideas for research

WANT to research—LOVE it (list research positions and what I've learned)

Learning data analysis techniques, computer programs

Love kids—summers spent at camp counseling when others worked at mall—shows leadership, independence

Spoke to Dr. Wheeler at USG about new ideas for effect of pet ownership on young children—plan on taking course in grief counseling

Dolphin training

Humane Society volunteer work

Earning money for college—hardworking, very dedicated and responsible

Won Student Leadership Award

Organized Eating Awareness Day

High math GREs

Strong GPA (especially in research and science courses)

Senior thesis (experience, paper, and defense)—"Effects of pet ownership vs. meditation on sleep in the elderly"

Work well with other people

OK, so what about *your* list? Give it a try here. What can you say about *you*, about your experience, credentials, interests, or characteristics that might somehow qualify you for graduate study?

_____
_____
_____
_____
_____
_____
_____
_____
_____

Now that you've taken that important first step, it's time to think about how to actually write the personal statement. Before you start writing, however, here are a few tips, some do's and don'ts, so that you don't have to go back and recast the entire structure or approach:

❖ DON'TS

1. *Don't write an autobiography.* Sometimes, students trying to find a way into the personal statement will start telling a story, which is fair enough, but they *keep* telling it! Instead of using just a brief anecdote, they will begin at the beginning ("I was born in Cleveland, Ohio"), progress to the middle ("When I was 11, we moved to California"), head toward the end ("I became interested in psychology after taking a high school AP course")—and continue on, and on, and on ("Your graduate school will help me achieve my dreams"). In this type of essay, called "My Name Is Bob Smith," the writer just doesn't know how to stop or what to focus on. As a result, the structure is purely chronological—this happened, then this, then this—and consequently a point cannot be made about much of anything. The personal statement becomes just a collection of equally important events unraveling in time. Therefore, when following the advice to "tell a story," tell a very *short* story, one that illustrates something. The point → avoid writing a personal statement that skims over your life from birth to the present.

2. *Don't write the form of autobiography known as "By Default."* Sometimes, students get on an autobiographical roll, telling first about how they tried all kinds of other majors and, by process of elimination, arrived at psychology as a major: "I took science courses so I could become a doctor, but as my transcripts show, I wasn't terribly good at chemistry. So I thought I'd try physical therapy because it seemed related to medicine, but I discovered it wasn't, so I completely changed direction and took humanities courses in history, art, and religion. Although these courses weren't specific enough for me, I did learn that the world's religions answer an inner need shared by all people, so I took a course in psychology to find out what else individuals might have in common. After just one course, psychology sparked my interest. I was hooked!" The point → who cares? (By the way, don't use the phrase "sparked my interest" or the word "hooked.")

3. *Don't write something too personal, or only personal.* This essay is not the place to discuss your friend's nervous breakdown; neither is it the place to claim that because members of your family have experienced mental illness you are therefore a good candidate for graduate school. Past problems, yours or someone else's, may make you empathetic, compassionate, and well acquainted with certain hands-on issues in the field, but your strength as a candidate is based on whether you can walk in

and do the work, not on whether you have had great misfortunes in your life. The point → avoid casting personal or family misfortunes or problems as *credentials*. Misfortunes, as far as admission to graduate school is concerned, may be meaningful and say something important about your tenacity, determination, or endurance, but they aren't in the same category as a high GPA, strong GREs, or research experience.

4. *Don't approach graduate school as therapy.* Students sometimes have powerful prior experiences that motivate them to pursue graduate school in order to understand themselves and other people (including their family members). A close cousin to 3, this type of personal statement typically devolves into a soul-searching treatise, with the applicant looking to graduate school as a way to make sense of past troubles and make earlier experiences meaningful or sensible in some way. However, graduate programs are not primarily in the business of helping students repair their lives. The point → understand that you are applying to be trained, not treated. Knowing the difference is vital to your getting into (and through) your graduate program.

5. *Don't dwell on the negative.* As long as we're talking about misfortune, consider this: if you have a brief anecdote to tell about the nervous breakdown mentioned earlier, fine, but be brief and don't dwell on the negative aspects of the experience, recounting event by event the crises that led to, say, institutionalization. Instead, move directly into the positive: you chose this story for a reason. Chances are that you learned something from it. What, specifically, did you learn? Suddenly, the misfortune has taken on another light altogether: it's been instructive. The point → if you are writing about a hardship or obstacle, if you are using an anecdote involving tragedy, spend at least as much space on the page explaining what you have taken away from the experience as you do in describing it.

6. *Don't editorialize.* Sometimes students hope that making philosophical pronouncements will accomplish the following:
- Make them sound smart and knowledgeable
- Reveal their position on a topic
- Show they understand the central issues in psychology and life

Consequently, statements such as "In today's world of impersonal technology, violence, and fragmented relationships, it is important to understand that everyone needs to have another person to talk to" find their way into personal statements. Often, in desperation, students fall back on such sentences for transition or filler, but the effect is unfortunate. Why? Because, let's face it, you are probably young, and you are applying to a graduate training program in order to learn about the field; making profound statements or pronouncements about psychology is something you should avoid just now. Wait until you've become older, more seasoned, and are among friends in an informal setting, gabbing about life in general. By then, you will also know what topics to expound on in certain company and what topics to avoid, such as politics and religion. The point → a personal statement is just that—*personal*—although, as we mentioned earlier, not *too* personal or *only* personal. The vita presents facts on a page; the personal statement is your one opportunity to make those facts come alive. What kind of a person are you? How well do you write—with wit and humor, with elegant prose? What sense do you make of your experience? What do you emphasize or downplay? How do you look at things? Every sentence should be about you or somehow related to you, because the admissions committee wants to know one thing: why *you* are an ideal candidate for the rigors of graduate work in their program.

7. *Don't tell the admissions committee about their school or resort to flattery.* You've done your homework, and you know all about the program to which you are applying, so it makes sense for you to convey that expertise and interest in the context of *good match* and *great fit*. But avoid sentences that could be interpreted as flattery, platitudes, or both: "Magnum University, outstanding for its national reputation, is ranked first for its graduate program in counseling by the National Council on Counseling Programs," or "The University of Minnesota has one of the best programs in the country, with outstanding faculty and an excellent reputation." Consider your audience: the people sitting on admissions committees already know how wonderful their institution is; they don't need you to tell them. By resorting to flattery, you run the risk of implying that you know only general information about the school (that it's great), but not the specifics you should know about the program itself. The point → use the limited number of words you have available to tell those deciding your future something they don't already know—and don't tell them what *you* think they want to hear, either!

❖ DO'S

Now let's focus on what you *should* do:

1. *Show, don't tell.* When you are selecting the raw material for your personal statement, and after you have heard from a variety of people about your strengths (and weaknesses), you will fashion

a person, think of a point, a theme, an impression. You might walk away from all your reflection with the idea, for example, that you are a hardworking and indomitable person, someone who pursues goals no matter what. Return to the reasons you have for thinking so. The reasons themselves are what should go into the personal statement. In other words, you want examples, concrete details, specific illustrations, not something along the lines of the following 52 words a person once used to describe himself:

> I am a very hardworking and determined individual who will not give up easily. I always choose the hardest courses, the longest work hours, the most credit hours that I can manage. I apply myself diligently to all that I do, because I believe that effort, work, and industry can accomplish anything.

Those 52 words said next to nothing, but consider the next 55 words:

> Despite taking courses in physics, chemistry, and anatomy, I still manage to work 30 hours a week in order to help pay my college expenses, and I also volunteer five hours a week at the shelter for battered women. If I'm not actively involved in some meaningful activity, I feel like I'm wasting my time.

Because of the courses named and the hours stipulated, the reader understands what those hard courses and credit hours actually are; most important, however, the reader draws the conclusion, "What a hardworking and industrious person!" Instead of being *told*, in other words, that the writer is hardworking and industrious, the reader is *shown* examples of determination and industry. So, instead of describing an important influence or event in your life (e.g., volunteering one spring for Habitat for Humanity), *illustrate* what you mean.

Telling	*Showing*
That spring, volunteering for Habitat for Humanity was the most important, life-changing experience I have ever had. We all worked so hard, from morning to night, and we didn't have time to do anything else. We were cold most of the time, and many of us got injured on the job.	In Harrisburg that spring, we bruised our knuckles, went hungry, and got sore and cold, but we rebuilt a staircase, installed new windows, painted halls, hung drywall, and made a home for a family that lived in a tent. For us, the reward was immense.

The point → don't be vague and general and leave out details. Use those details to create a picture so that the reader can conclude, rather than have you draw conclusions ("We all worked so hard").

2. *Mention opportunities you have taken advantage of, or extra work you've done, or responsibilities you've assumed.* If, for example, you took a graduate course because you needed the extra stimulation or wanted to find out what such courses are like, make sure you make a point of saying so in the personal statement. Likewise, if you wrote a thesis, the personal statement is the perfect place to explain what you learned, because its inclusion on the vita is only a one-line entry, just like a graduate course. The point → some vitally important information will appear only as a blip on the vita; make sure you spend a little time in your personal statement expanding on whatever distinguishes you from the next applicant.

3. *Mention that you've contacted a member of the department or that you've read so-and-so's article.* Suppose you are fascinated by the phenomenon of familial homicide. Try to contact a member of the department whose work on the subject you admire. Even if you can't actually reach that person, mention that you've read his or her article on matricide and find it illuminating because you, too, hope to study familial homicide. Note that this contact or this reading reflects sincere interest and is not simply an attempt to "earn points." Few things raise eyebrows faster than a personal statement that lists half the faculty as potentially interesting to work with, as in "I could easily see myself working with Dr. Smith, Dr. Jones, Dr. White, Dr. Marone, or Dr. Blanco." The faculty mentioned may have few, if any, interests in common, and nominating all of them as your potential advisors or mentors actually muddies the waters rather than clarifies your interests. After all, with whom, exactly, would you work, and how would the faculty determine that on the basis of your statement? The point → if you've gotten in touch with someone in the department, mention that you've done so. E-mailing faculty ahead of time can be valuable. You would be surprised at how many students receive e-mail responses from professors interested in talking about their work and how eagerly these faculty members approach the review of candidates who have maintained contact with them over time.

4. *Suggest that you can contribute something to the program.* In general, students zero in on what the school can do for them, forgetting that they will enter a reciprocal relationship with that institution. The point → you might sound self-absorbed if you say something like

"A degree from X University, which has the best child-clinical psychology program in the country, will allow me to pursue my dream of becoming a successful practitioner." What can *you* do for X University? Maybe nothing spectacular right now, but at least don't suggest you are the only one standing to benefit. Programs build their reputations, in part, by the quality and number of their graduate students. Potential graduate students are attracted to institutions with good reputations. The relationship is reciprocal.

❖ STRUCTURING THE PERSONAL STATEMENT

There are many ways to organize a personal statement. When in doubt, however, try the *past–present–future model*. Beginning with the past allows you to recount a story, mention a pivotal event, quote your grandfather, or discuss an experience that changed your life, such as moving 15 times in 10 years. Of course, that first streamlined and vibrantly written paragraph has to invite the reader into the second paragraph, which focuses on the present, which for you is undergraduate school. This natural movement takes you right into your undergraduate career—the courses you've taken and what you've learned about yourself through them, the volunteer experience that required all your time, energy, and stamina, and so forth. From there, the organic unfolding leads directly to the future: Why does X University have the perfect graduate program for you? With whom will you work? What have you done to prepare for graduate school?

It's easy to see why, in general, the past–present–future model is all purpose in nature:

1. It allows you to begin by telling a story or anecdote:

    When I was five years old, my best friend would return from visiting his father with bruises around his face and on his arms, injuries that he claimed he got by climbing a tree, riding a bike, or playing football. After awhile, these stories didn't ring true, so I pressed him, and he started to cry, telling me that his father would "get mad" at the stupid little things he did, like tripping on the edge of the rug or spilling milk. Coming from a peaceful and trusting family, I was horrified and immediately told my father what I had heard. Though my memory of subsequent events is unclear, I do recall one thing: my best friend's beatings stopped, and my father said I had done the right thing by telling him. Now, I can identify this experience in my young life as a turning point: I suddenly understood the absolute value of intervention, and all these years later know why I am so committed to pursuing a career in counseling psychology.

These 172 words (perhaps too many) accomplish a great deal: we know the writer, as a child, had a friend who was abused but rescued, in part, by the writer's intercession. Instead of focusing on the horror of child abuse or the importance of a trusting and safe family, the writer mentions the unpleasant incident, conveys its very important effect on him, and is positioned to move on to a new paragraph emphasizing the present. Indeed, such a powerful experience proved to be the impetus for the writer choosing his direction in life. So we learn a lot about the applicant in a relatively short space, but let's see if we can't trim those 172 words down, so that they don't constitute almost one third of the essay:

When I was five, my best friend visited his father on weekends, often returning with bruises he claimed to have gotten by falling off his bike or out of a tree. After awhile his stories began to sound fishy, so I pressed him, and he started to cry, telling me he got "punished" for doing stupid things, like spilling his milk. Coming from a peaceful and trusting family, I couldn't understand that kind of punishment, so I told my father, and although my memory of subsequent events is unclear, my friend's beatings stopped. Now, almost 20 years later, I can identify this experience in my young life as a turning point: I suddenly realized the absolute value of intervention and understand why I am so committed to pursuing a career in counseling psychology.

The paragraph now has 133 words, with the same powerful anecdote and the same point about pursuing a career in counseling psychology, and the writer has some 40 extra words to use elsewhere.

2. The past–present–future model offers a ready-made format for you to talk about your undergraduate preparation and experience—the present, in other words. If we continue with our first example, the one about the child who told his dad about the friend's abuse, the present might look something like this:

During high school, I took the Advanced Placement course in Psychology, received an A, earned additional college credits in a dual-enrollment program with Howdy Community College,

50 THE VIRTUAL ADVISOR

> and began classes at the University of Florida with sophomore standing. I immediately enrolled in as many psychology courses as I could while fulfilling my other requirements, and in less than a year, having become certified in crisis counseling, was also ready to take every upper division psychology course the department offered. Certain of those courses—Eating Disorders, Abnormal Psychology, and Constructivist Psychology—led to my close association with Dr. Smith, whose laboratory I joined in the spring of my junior year. Instead of graduating in three years, I decided to take advantage of the full four so I could continue working on Dr. Smith's research into the relationship of narcissistic personality disorder and kleptomania. Furthermore, in another of his laboratories, I became the head research assistant in a project titled "Attachment Theory and the Development of Critical Thinking Skills." My senior thesis, in fact, is derived from data sets collected in this laboratory.

With a certain breathiness indicating his whirlwind academic career, the writer moves into the present, with passing reference to high school, emphasizing the development of his interest, skills, direction, his research relationship with Dr. Smith, and his thesis topic.

3. The past–present–future model allows you to glide into the conclusion: what graduate school you want to attend, who you want to work with there, and why you are well suited to be chosen. If we continue with our preceding example, the writer, in about 300 words pertaining to the past and present, is poised to head into the future:

> I am fortunate in having known from such an early age the direction my life would take: I never wavered in my desire and determination to understand and ultimately contribute to the body of knowledge on human behavior. Specifically, I seek to pursue graduate studies under Dr. Jones at X University, and I have been in touch with her regarding her recent groundbreaking research on approaches to counseling that include the five-step method of assessing trust. Because of my thorough training in crisis counseling, as well as my solid background in research, I feel certain I can contribute to Dr. Jones's investigations by further examining the relationship of critical thinking skills to trust. I also believe that my extensive coursework, my honors GPA, my single-mindedness, and my familiarity with the complexities and pitfalls of research

all demonstrate that I am a mature and serious student, ready to take on the rigors of graduate work at X University, my first choice among graduate schools.

In about 500 words, this student has accomplished the following:

- Said how he got interested in psychology
- Shown a personal side through his choice of anecdotes (his compassion for a friend, his own family solidarity, his trust and empathy, his ability to take action)
- Demonstrated drive (he zipped through high school and college)
- Convinced the reader of his strong sense of direction (he's been committed to this field forever, and in fact took one extra year of college to explore it)
- Maintained a high GPA (mentioned in passing, along with the thesis)
- Engaged actively in research with one professor
- Became certified in crisis counseling

As readers, we consequently believe this writer when he makes his pitch for X University, especially because he's been in contact with someone whose research he's read and has specific plans to extend. The writer demonstrates an understanding of "fit"—that is, he has read about the school and knows what his role could be working under a faculty member he names as having contacted. Although this personal statement is nothing spectacular, it nevertheless gets the job done by tying the conclusion to the introduction, by conveying a long-standing and serious commitment to the field, and by demonstrating the discipline needed to succeed in that field. In other words, it connects the dots and answers the critical question: "what would this student bring to our program?"

❖ THIS AND THAT

Here are some important points to keep in mind when fashioning your personal statement. Although there are no "rights" and "wrongs," there are some things that are "better" or "worse."

1. *Explain weaknesses.* The personal statement can be used to mention, in passing, grades from a bad semester, or the fact that you withdrew for a semester or have marginal GREs—in other words, if you

think some explaining is needed, by all means, clarify here, but DO NOT MAKE EXCUSES. Sometimes a dependent clause will do the trick: "Although my fall semester sophomore year grades reflect my confusion over which career path to pursue, since that period I have consistently made the dean's list and in fact will graduate with honors in my chosen field." Make sure you turn the negative into a positive: "Although I had to withdraw spring semester of my junior year because my parents could no longer afford to pay tuition, I have since returned, stronger than ever now that I have a part-time job that helps defray expenses." Or, "Although I have not completed any formal research experience, this fact is deceptive. I did take an advanced laboratory course where we critiqued published studies and drafted papers using American Psychological Association style, and I also completed an additional Research Methods course, during which I first began to review the literature on the topic of sleep disorders, now my primary area of interest."

2. *Work with the facts.* The personal statement should not raise questions but answer them. If your epiphany took place in high school, but you suggest that moment of insight occurred during your junior year of college, the alert reader will wonder what's going on. Another way of making this point is: be completely honest. Don't try to fool the admissions committee by being deceptive or too clever.

3. *Don't pad or add.* Don't pad the personal statement or exaggerate your accomplishments. We know a person who claimed membership in a local band, when all he did was bang the tambourine during one performance of a short-lived group. Imagine what might have happened if he had gotten an interview and was asked about that local band!

4. *Don't repeat again.* Don't simply repeat what's in your vita by converting listings into complete sentences. Instead, if you need to refer to your extensive research experience, but actually want to elaborate on something else, simply say, "As my vita indicates, I have extensive research experience." The point of the personal statement is to convey a sense of the *person* behind those experiences, skills, honors, and awards.

5. *Listen up!* Have someone read your personal statement aloud to you. When *you* read what you've written, you anticipate what comes next because you put those words there. Consequently, anticipation interferes with your ability to judge objectively the actual quality of the prose as it condenses your life into 500 words. However, listening comprehension is another faculty altogether: hearing your personal statement will enable you to discern words, phrases, and sentences that sound off register.

In fact, you may decide to move whole sentences and paragraphs around once you've heard someone else represent you in another voice entirely.

❖ STYLE: WRITING VIBRANT, LIVELY PROSE

All advice on creating the personal statement emphasizes the importance of good writing. But what does that mean, and how can you write well, especially if you consider yourself merely mediocre when it comes to composing text? First, there are things NOT to do. Do not have errors in your personal statement, and do not have extraneous words. Then there are things you should do: vary your sentence structure, use original diction instead of canned words and phrases, and avoid the passive voice.

Applicants are judged, at least implicitly, on how well they communicate, because graduate school and subsequent professional activities require that you write often and well. Therefore, the better you write now, the better your chances are to be admitted to graduate school, where you will further use your strong writing skills. A good writer gets the attention of an admissions committee every time, believe us! Don't worry; there's actually a bit of a formula to good writing. Here are some things to consider.

Vary Sentence Structure

In lively, vibrant prose, sentence structure is varied to make your language snappy, muscular, invigorated, and crisp. When you concentrate on varying sentence structure (in perhaps the third revision or so), you will find that you also trim extraneous words and eliminate the omnipresent *I* of the personal statement. Consider the following paragraph in an early draft of a personal statement before it was subjected to the vibrant, vivid prose test:

> I am a strong candidate for your program because I have a solid background in research. I worked for one semester coding data, observing behavior, and conducting literature reviews for a study on pigeons. I also maintained the laboratory and experimental animals, ordered materials, and reported anomalous behaviors. I learned a great deal about the complexity of protocols, the importance of timely institutional review approval, and the necessity of precise record-keeping from this experience. This allowed me to apply for

> and be accepted by another lab the following semester. I trained additional undergraduate research assistants and supervised the procurement and care of genetically identical mice for a study on addiction. I joined a third lab in developmental psychology in order to learn how to administer baseline tests, conduct phone interviews, and interpret data from three semesters' worth of data collection.

This passage has several problems, most notably—it's boring! Sounding like it's been written in a monotone, these 140 words drone on because the writer begins virtually every sentence with *I* and follows that pronoun with a verb and an object. Even though the information conveys competence, that competence is undercut by the writer's lack of enthusiasm and imagination. So let's revise!

> My solid background in three research laboratories has prepared me for the rigors of graduate work. First, in a project investigating the effects of token reinforcement on pigeons, I coded data and observed behaviors, learning how to be patient and precise in experimentation and how to recognize anomalous behaviors. As the person responsible for maintaining this lab, its animals and supplies, I also learned the vital importance of correct animal care and a clean, well-stocked environment. Following this experience, which introduced me to the complexity of protocols and precise record-keeping, I was fortunate to join a second lab studying addiction, where I trained other undergraduates in the procedures involved in caring for the genetically identical mice I was responsible for procuring. Finally, to add another dimension to my background in the field, I joined a third lab that taught me very different skills: how to administer baseline tests and conduct successful phone interviews that were subsequently transcribed and compiled into several semesters' worth of data, which I am now helping to analyze.

These 172 words not only add information about what the writer learned from each experience—something very important to do—but the use of *I* is trimmed down to six instances, whereas the first draft had seven, in 30 fewer words, no less! Also, not one of the sentences in the revision begins with *I*. Instead, each sentence begins somewhat differently, thus lessening the effect of the needed but redundant first-person singular pronoun. Another way to avoid the omnipresent *I* is to use compound verbs. Rather than the compound sentence "I volunteered at the women's shelter for six months, and I assisted at the crisis stabilization unit for another six months," recast the sentence thus: "I volunteered at the women's shelter for six months and at the crisis stabilization unit for another six months." By so doing, the use of *I* is cut by 50%, and two words are eliminated in the process.

Finally, the revised paragraph corrects the very mistaken use of *this*: "This allowed me to apply for and be accepted by another lab the following semester." *This* cannot refer to the several sentences or the general idea that preceded it. *This* can be used ONLY to refer to *this* computer, *this* graduate school, *this* day—to something specific, not to sweeping antecedents.

Why don't you give revision a try? Take the following sentences and refashion them by varying sentence structure. Feel free to inject some lively, vibrant prose, too. You want the reader to share the experience and become involved with it. Embellish the passage with other information, reactions, or experiences, as well. Your goal is to make it interesting and engaging, so give it a try!

> I participated in a laboratory in social psychology in my Junior year. It was directed by Dr. Stephens. I enjoyed the lab but wanted other experience, so I participated in another lab in my Senior year. It was directed by Dr. Mosher and it was in the area of developmental psychology. I learned a lot in both labs. I learned about psychology and about research methods. I administered questionnaires and I conducted interviews. I helped compile the data, too. I also helped one of the graduate students who was doing her dissertation. I learned that I like doing research from this experience and, as a result, I am excited about doing research in graduate school.

Now for your version:

_____
_____
_____
_____
_____
_____
_____
_____
_____

What differences do you see? Is your version longer, or shorter? Did you begin with something other than *I*? Did you use vibrant language? Is your version "punched up"? We sure hope so!

Original Diction

Watch out for the thesaurus. In fact, do not use one at all! Your own language is always best, because it's natural, but you must make an effort; really *think* about the best word to use. Don't just grab the first canned phrase or word that comes to mind and allow it to remain in that precious, once-in-a-lifetime document you are preparing. Minimize the use of the following stock words to describe yourself: *absorb(ed), ambitious, articulate, capable, competent, creative, detail oriented, determined, devoted, efficient, energetic, experienced, goal oriented, hard working, independent, knowledgeable, motivated, organized, participate in, proficient, reliable, skilled,* or *worthy.*

Avoid these canned words or expressions as well: *address the issue, amazing* (or *awesome*), *basically, bottom line, despite the fact that, discovered, due to, dream of, examine, facilitate, foundation in, engaged in, explore in depth, goal, exact same, involvement in, ongoing, prioritize,* and *pushing the envelope.*

Avoid ordinary modifiers, adjectives, and adverbs, either singly or in phrases: *enormous and lasting impact; challenging, fruitful, and fulfilling career; unusual in the respect that it seldom occurs; drastically and permanently affect the quality of a person's life.*

Passive Voice

Passive voice takes the agent, the doer, and puts it in the object position, as in the object of the preposition, and bumps the object of the preposition into the subject position. Compare the passive voice with the active voice in these examples:

Active voice: Roger hit the ball.

Passive voice: The ball was hit by Roger.

Notice the weird disconnectedness of the second sentence, which uses two more words than the first to suggest that Roger performed an action, but that bit of vital information is revealed only as the last word in the sentence. If Roger hit the ball, then Roger should take responsibility for it and be the subject of the sentence, as he is in active voice.

Crafting Your Personal Statement   57

Consider the ethereal, disembodied feel of the next few sentences, all in passive voice:

> The decision to enter psychology was made after a heartbreaking experience involving the loss of a sibling.
>
> During my sophomore year, there was an epiphany that allowed me to see the effect I could have on someone's life.
>
> The effect of counseling was felt after I resolved my differences with my sister.
>
> The idea that distance would teach me greater independence was arrived at after much discussion.

Rewritten in active voice, those sentences are much more direct and vigorous:

> I decided to major in psychology after my brother died.
>
> During sophomore year, I had an epiphany that showed me the effect I could have on someone's life.
>
> I felt the effect of counseling after resolving my differences with my sister.
>
> After much discussion, I understood that distance would teach me greater independence.

Notice how the second sentence in the following pairs is improved by slashing extraneous words:

> It was this experience that taught me the value of loyalty.
>
> *This experience taught me the value of loyalty.*
>
> The reason I have chosen psychology as a major is that I have always known I want to help people.
>
> *I am majoring in psychology in order to help people.*
>
> Volunteering has been an experience I enjoy.
>
> *I enjoy volunteering.*

The difference between passive and active voice can be subtle, but it's significant. Here are a couple of examples of sentences written in passive voice. Can you rewrite them in active voice? Practice revising here:

> During my sophomore year, an opportunity presented itself to me to join a laboratory in cognitive psychology.

_____

_____

_____

> The idea that psychology could become a career for me occurred following my participation in Dr. Marlboros's laboratory on smoking cessation.

_____

_____

_____

If you were the member of an admissions committee and you read a few hundred of these sorts of sentences, which would you prefer: yours (in the active voice), or those earlier ones (in the passive voice)?

In closing, by paying attention to the simple features we have outlined in this section on your personal statement, you will increase its impact and its effectiveness substantially. Two concluding points are worth emphasizing. First, there is no such thing as a "perfect" personal statement. So take your personal statement seriously, but don't obsess over its every word. Remember, it's not designed to gain you admission into graduate school, only to help get you an interview (a important subject dealt with at length in *The Online Advisor*). Have you painted a picture of yourself that would invite people to want to take a closer look? If your personal statement conveys a sense of you, presents your qualifications for graduate study, and establishes fit with that particular graduate program, then you are done. Mission accomplished. Second, don't forget that your personal statement is a companion piece to your vita. Between the two of them, you can cover all your bases, as long as you use your narrative ability well—start strong, explain what you've learned from specific experiences, and mention that you've contacted professors at the target school. By attending to even a portion of the things we have outlined in this section on personal statements, you will be way ahead of the pack, so good luck!

FEATURE

Q & A: The Personal Statement

Q: How "personal" should my personal statement be?

A: Your personal statement should present you as a person. It's the only piece in your application that speaks about you from your own perspective. It should help the reader get to know you and should convey qualities about you that are likely to be relevant to graduate school. It should not detail or dwell on personal trauma, dysfunction, or psychopathology. Your struggles with substance abuse, eating disorders, or depression may have helped cultivate your interest in psychology, but they do not represent qualifications or credentials for graduate study per se. Many students begin their personal statements by touching briefly on, for example, a painful or exhilarating experience, a turning point, an epiphany, but they move right on to academic qualifications.

Q: My personal statement overlaps with my vita. What should I do about that?

A: The personal statement and the vita serve different functions. The vita telegraphs your qualifications for graduate study, whereas the personal statement weaves them into a narrative account. It signals what you have learned from these experiences, personally, and how they have helped to transform you and your directions in relation to the programs to which you are applying. In short, the personal statement uses selected parts of your vita to tell a compelling story about how you, your experiences, and your interests fit with a particular graduate program. Don't worry about overlap in content between the two. Even though they may contain some of the same information, they present that information in different ways from different perspectives.

Q: At what point in my life should I start my personal statement?

A: There is no single best point; people approach the narrative differently. Most students begin somewhere in college, when their interests first begin to take shape, but others note critical experiences in high school that helped inform their current interests, represent longstanding passions, or both. Remember, there are lots of different ways that you could accomplish the same purpose, which is to outline how you have developed your particular interests and how they match with the programs to which you are applying.

(Continued)

(Continued)

> **Q:** Shouldn't my personal statement sound "smart"? I'm applying to a graduate program, after all.
>
> **A:** Your intelligence is reflected in a number of ways. You have your GRE, your GPA, and what your letter writers have to say about you, for starters. So there is little need to sound "smart" in your personal statement. What you want most to sound like is yourself, because the central question your readers will be asking is, "What is this person like, and what would it be like to work with him or her?"
>
> **Q:** How long should my personal statement be?
>
> **A:** It should be long enough to cover the subject, but short enough to make it interesting! Most personal statements are a couple of pages long. Yours will be given only two to three minutes to read, so there is no sense in writing five pages. Don't forget, it's not an autobiography!

FEATURE

Words of Wisdom From Successful Graduate Applicants

Find a balance between being professional and conveying your personhood in the personal statement. This is your opportunity to share you and what makes you unique. This is your chance to tell the programs about yourself and why you would be a great addition to their program. Keep in mind that this should be done in a professional way, however. Telling a program that you are interested in psychology because of your 10 years in intensive psychotherapy probably is not the way to go. Instead, talk about your path in psychology and what brought you to where you are with regard to your interest in obtaining a graduate degree and/or your research interests. —Sara R.

It is not easy writing an effective personal statement. I went through several drafts and still felt like I could have done a better job. I would recommend [starting] early, and make sure to show your drafts to your mentor or a professor. Have them give you some feedback that can steer you in a better direction. Make sure to have someone read for consistency and clarity. I believe most admissions committees want you to get straight to the point so start off by stating why you are applying to their program. Personal experiences are great to add, but don't overdo it. —Mark M.

FEATURE

Success Stories and Personal Statements

#1. If At First You Don't Succeed . . .

One year, a female student applied to several graduate programs and was turned down by all of them, even though she easily exceeded their stated requirements; her credentials were excellent. Discouraged, she went to New York, worked as a nanny (this person is not the nanny mentioned earlier), and reapplied to graduate school, including several of the ones she had been rejected by before. Not expecting much, she was ecstatic to find she had been accepted by the school she most wanted to attend; it was one of those that had declined her previous application. Why was she accepted the second time around? Was it because of her nanny experience? Because she applied again? Because her personal statement (the only part of her application that changed) was better? It's hard to say, but one thing to remember when you apply to graduate school—perhaps the most important thing in terms of your self-esteem and sanity—is that your application is considered among many others. One year, yours may appear lackluster because the applicant pool is remarkably strong, and another year that same application may place you at the top of the heap. Try to put your application in perspective: applicant pools vary from year to year. There is a great deal of relativity built into this process: you may be lucky, or you may not.

#2. What Are Your Strengths?

After graduating college with a degree in psychology, this student became a flight attendant but decided several years later that she really wanted to go to graduate school for a PhD. So she sat down and thought long and hard about her credentials, which seemed to her deficient because her undergraduate experience had ended years earlier. What qualifications did she have, she wondered, that would make her competitive with other applicants having lots of research experience, high GREs, and so forth. As it turned out, the very thing this person worried about was her greatest strength: she had been out of school for a few years dealing with all kinds of people in a fairly high-stress environment, handling various crises, juggling a difficult schedule, and coping with a cross-section of travelers, all of whom were anxious, impatient, angry, addled, distracted, hurried, and emotional. This person made the most of what she had to offer; she wrote about how being a mature individual with years' worth of real-world experience of the kind mentioned earlier qualified her for graduate school. She was admitted—perhaps not entirely because of her personal statement, but that essay certainly reflected the kind of self-scrutiny necessary to build a case for acceptance.

(Continued)

(Continued)

#3. Diving Into Graduate Study

This student was a superb scuba diver who had just decided to become a psychology major. In his junior year, he began to think about graduate school. But he had no laboratories, no volunteer experience, no fieldwork—nothing to substantiate his claim that he would make an outstanding graduate student in psychology. What he did have, however, when he wrote his personal statement, were several different certifications in cave diving and open water diving, because this sport had been his passion for years. How could he use this unusual and extensive experience to make a case for himself as a graduate student in psychology?

After mulling this history over and creating many drafts, he realized that sometimes, during tight situations underwater, he had encountered firsthand much of what he was currently studying—that is, scuba diving had prepared him for the textbooks of psychology in a most remarkable way. As he read about panic attacks, for example, he could relate directly to the material because he'd had a dive partner who once suddenly and unexpectedly experienced one. As this student read about other phenomena, he was able to connect them to what he knew about diving. The effects of binge drinking and the effects of diving too deep on compressed air and suffering nitrogen narcosis—the "rapture of the deep"—were similar, he realized. The bizarre behavior of afflicted divers who have sometimes been seen offering their regulators to fish was, in fact, a form of serious drunkenness. Once this student made the connections between diving and psychology, he was off and running with his personal statement. He had a hook that allowed him to develop a distinctive, memorable, and effective personal statement, drawing from an area of experience that was important to him.

4

Securing Your Letters of Recommendation

❖ ❖ ❖

In This Chapter You Will Learn:

- ❖ How and when to ask for letters
- ❖ What to give professors to help them write the strongest letter possible
- ❖ How to make yourself memorable to professors
- ❖ The importance of organization and thoroughness

The first thing to remember about applying to graduate school is that it's a process. You don't just wake up one day and start your applications, which have magically appeared on your desk, ready to be filled out. The process begins the moment you decide to become a psychology major, if not before. Securing letters of recommendation highlights this fact; these letters are cultivated across time, not solicited at the last moment. So in this chapter we focus on how to obtain letters of recommendation and what you can do to maximize their value to you.

It needs to be stated clearly from the outset that good letters of recommendation can make or break your application. Among all the components of your graduate application, letters of recommendation have consistently been found to carry the greatest weight. If you have borderline GREs, a marginal GPA, or minimal research experience, strong letters can compensate for that shortcoming and earn you an interview or acceptance. Plus, more than any other component of your graduate application, letters of recommendation speak directly to your capacity for graduate work, and they do so from the perspective of faculty members just like the ones making the decision to admit you or not. Therefore, do not take obtaining letters lightly.

When you think about your letters of recommendation, think about them individually and collectively. Individually, you want each one to be excellent; collectively, you want them to speak to the full range of your relevant skills or experiences. In other words, like the old Gestalt maxim that "the whole is greater than the sum of the parts," each of your letters should complement the other letters. Individually, you want each of your letters to address important aspects of your skills and experiences as they relate to your graduate programs. For example, if you are applying for a master's degree in general experimental psychology, you might want a letter from a professor who taught you Research Methods, a faculty member with whom you did research, or the professor who supervised your senior thesis. On the other hand, if you are applying to a child–clinical program, you may want someone who can speak to your experience in working with children, as well as someone who has supervised your research.

Your letter writers ideally will represent the full range of your experience relevant to the graduate programs to which you are applying. For a research-oriented program you need letter writers who can speak to your research skills; for a professional program you need letter writers who can speak to your professional skills; for a science–practice program, you need letter writers who can address both of these domains. Collectively, then, your recommenders will assuredly comment on some of the same qualities (those personal characteristics that will serve you in good stead in graduate school), so your letters will strengthen and confirm each other even while they address different domains of experience (coursework, research experiences, community settings). In other words, they will form a Gestalt.

So now let's explore how you can go about cultivating relationships with your potential letter writers so that you will have a number of references to choose from when the time comes to apply for graduate schools. During your coursework, you no doubt had favorite professors or most-loved classes. The first step in obtaining letters of recommendation is, therefore:

Take note of good courses, good professors, your own performance, and opportunities to make personal contact.

Students often wait until the beginning of their senior year to review their academic careers, wondering which professors to ask for letters of recommendation. By then, it's very late in the game, so try to identify, as you go along, exactly *who* would say *what* about you. Suppose you took a large lecture course in Abnormal Psychology. You had a teaching assistant (TA) for section, but you loved the professor, who was funny, engaging, knowledgeable, and inspiring. You saw this faculty member only during his or her fabulous weekly lectures. However, the class was so riveting that you found yourself studying hard even though you were taking more than the regular courseload, and you did exceptionally well on the examinations because of your dedication. After taking the course, in which you received a high A, you are now considering graduate study in counseling psychology, largely because of the content and presentation of the Abnormal Psychology material and the fact that the professor was a counseling psychologist. Two semesters have passed, and you wonder if this professor would be a good person to ask for a letter because, according to your reasoning, (1) he or she changed your life: you have decided to go to graduate school in counseling psychology; and (2) you got a great grade in the class.

There is nothing wrong with your reasoning per se, but you have stumbled on the problem facing many students. The classes that influence or interest you are sometimes taught by professors in large lectures, and the person you have come to know is the TA, not the professor. One question students frequently ask is, "Is it all right for a TA to write a letter?" The answer to the question is "yes" and "no." Yes, because it is not unusual for students to begin senior year acquainted with only one or two faculty members but needing three letters of recommendation. If you are one of those students, you might return to the Abnormal Psychology TA and ask for advice. That person, theoretically, would then speak to the professor or tell you to visit him or her. Indeed, some professors write letters through their TAs—that is, the TA might draft a letter remarking on your outstanding potential, and the professor would review, edit, and sign the letter. Seldom, if ever, however, does the TA write and sign off on a letter from start to finish, and definitely not in the name of the professor. So our "yes" response has certain qualifications, some of which apply to letters of recommendations in general:

- Try to have your letters come from people with the highest degree possible, preferably someone with a doctorate.

- Never have a family friend write a letter attesting to your good character.

- Use letters from community or outside professional sources selectively; if you have worked for a psychologist in some capacity—for example, over several summers—then that person might be able to say certain good things about you, if you are applying to a professional program, that is.

Remember, letters of recommendation carry great weight in application decisions, so choose your recommenders wisely and early. If you must ask a TA for a letter, then go ahead, but ideally you should have worked for that TA in a laboratory, stayed in touch with him or her after the class ended, or know that person well. Then the TA, who presumably still works with the professor, can in good conscience approach that professor on your behalf. However, returning two semesters after a course has ended to ask a TA to help you get a letter might well result in a deadly lukewarm recommendation or a downright refusal. Therefore, "no" in response to "Is it all right for a TA to write a letter?" begins here.

No, it is not a good idea to ask a TA to write a letter, for this important reason:

A letter of recommendation attests to your ability to perform graduate work; a TA is a graduate student performing graduate work. Therefore, a TA is generally not in a position to comment on your ability to function in graduate school.

But if you tackle this potential problem ahead of time, it is easy to address. Here's how. During the hypothetical Abnormal Psychology course discussed earlier, establish contact with the professor at that time, rather than waiting two semesters. In other words, be proactive! Then you won't have to ask a TA for a letter of recommendation, because you've positioned yourself to ask the professor directly. Here are some suggestions for getting to know your professors, who, despite what you might think, actually welcome visits from students. Each suggestion is followed by a space for you to jot notes in response to the question asked:

1. *Go to office hours.* We are always astonished at how few students take advantage of this time to ask questions. The students who do come, for whatever reason, are almost always the good students, memorable because they took the time to introduce themselves and manifest some

curiosity about the assignments or some aspect of the course. Name the professors whose office hours you've already taken advantage of, then name three you think you might like to visit:

_____

_____

_____

_____

_____

2. *Do not find excuses **not** to go to office hours*: "I have nothing to say," "Oh, the professor is so busy, he or she won't want me to take up valuable time," "That professor is known to be cranky, scary, unavailable, disinterested, etc." Your challenge is to find a reason to drop by. If you are truly interested in the material, so interested that you set aside other courses and nights out to study for the tests, then finding something to talk about shouldn't be a problem. And you don't have to stay for an hour; a 10-minute meeting speaks volumes about your interest, your dedication, and your initiative—all important qualities in a graduate student. Start by asking simple things. Ask for further readings on a particular topic relevant to the course. Ask the professor what additional courses might follow logically from the current one he or she is teaching. Ask questions that arise naturally from reading the text. Ask for advice about related courses, or courses the professor might teach in the future. Some students are reluctant to go to office hours because they think it's "brown-nosing." On the contrary, if you hope to become a professional, it makes sense to engage current professionals in professional discussions now. Hundreds of students come and go, taking psychology courses just to fulfill requirements or to satisfy their curiosity, but psychology majors intent on graduate school are unique, and faculty especially value their contact with these individuals. So start now by viewing these office visits as part of your preprofessional development. What are the office hours of the professors you listed above?

_____

_____

_____

_____

_____

3. *During the course, or immediately after, tell the professor how much you learned and how much you enjoyed the course.* It may surprise you to hear that, as hardworking as professors are, not many students actually take the time to say thanks, or "Well done." It's not currying favor to express gratitude; neither is it "sucking up" to pursue intellectual interests. Your professors need a way to know and remember you so that they can vouch for your curiosity, drive, ability—the qualities that distinguish you as someone more than likely to excel in graduate school. They also need to know firsthand that they've done a good job. It feels good to be appreciated—and the person who takes the time to express that appreciation will be remembered. Name three courses you particularly liked, and what you liked about them:

_____

_____

_____

4. *If you truly love the subject area, ask the professor if he or she needs help running a study*—but do your homework ahead of time. Know what your favorite professor, the one you're dropping by to see, is up to at the moment. You might be surprised to find that professors are often eager to enlist help on projects. You could volunteer to work in any capacity. (Another way to gain research or laboratory experience is to faithfully scan the bulletin boards in your department and visit the advising office and the online postings regularly.) Identify one professor you are willing to do anything to help:

_____

5. *Go to departmental functions and talks that interest you.* Your favorite professor might be there as well. Strike up a conversation afterward. You might also mention the graduate schools you're interested in or the specific areas of research that fascinate you, because occasionally one professor can send you to another in the department who knows someone else at another school. Sometimes, also, the professor you are speaking to stays in touch with a faculty member who knows someone somewhere. In other words, by talking to one professor, during office hours or at departmental functions, you increase your opportunities to gain access to the individuals whose interests correspond to your own. Those people, in turn, might prove to be valuable resources

Securing Your Letters of Recommendation   69

to you. Name two upcoming events, along with the place, time, and date, that interest you:

_____

_____

6. *Read articles by the professor you plan on visiting.* By doing so, you will be sure to have a topic of conversation or a question to ask. Applying to graduate school is all about doing your homework. If you aren't prepared or willing to conduct lots of informal research now, perhaps you might consider another career choice. List two articles by the professor whose office hours you now know and plan on taking advantage of:

_____

_____

7. *Ask questions about test results.* As you know by now, checking why you missed a question is one of the surest ways to learn something, so drop by during office hours to find out what you missed on an assignment and why. If your assignment was a paper, so much the better! You have lots to talk about if you got a B+. By taking this step, you show your professor that you want to do your very best. Your goal is not to protest your grade but to understand the basis for it and how you can do better. This determination demonstrates emotional maturity and a dedication to the pursuit of excellence, two vital qualities in graduate school success.

Question 1: _____

Question 2: _____

8. *Introduce yourself after the first or second class.* In a large lecture setting, getting to know individual students is next to impossible for professors, who do in fact value knowing their students individually. So personalize the contact as soon as you can. Go up after class and say "I want to introduce myself," give your name, and indicate that you are looking forward to the course. It's that simple.

Last, immediately after the course is over, ask the professor if she or he is willing to write a *strong* letter of recommendation for you when the time comes. If you have followed the steps outlined earlier throughout the semester, the professor by now recognizes you, realizes you are interested in the area, and probably knows that you are considering graduate study in the field. By asking for a recommendation, you are telling that professor something more—and gauging his or her reaction at the same time. So watch the response carefully. In other words, during this conversation your radar should be turned on high. Pay attention to the nuances. Sniff out enthusiasm. Your professor, who by now also knows you well, will say something like:

1. "Of course! I'd love to!"
2. "Ask me again when the time comes."
3. "I will be on sabbatical then."
4. "If you can't find someone whose research interests are more in line with yours, then come back, and I will."
5. "I've already promised too many people."

There are other possible responses, of course, but if you get a lively 1 or its equivalent, then you're set. If the response is a 2, then you're probably on safe ground; a 3 is worth pursuing. (You might clarify how you might get in touch with the on-leave professor.) If the response is a 4 or a 5, however, you might consider asking someone else less overcommitted or ambivalent. On occasion, faculty members may feel that they do not know you well enough to write a strong letter on your behalf. Keep in mind that you are not being personally rejected; some professors have a policy regarding letters of recommendation: they will write letters only for students who work in their laboratories. Even bright, talented, capable students who have taken multiple classes with them may not get letters.

By the way, just so you know what professors have to assess you according to—and why TAs aren't qualified to write letters for prospective peers—the required forms that accompany the letters of recommendation contain some version of the following categories, which have to be checked in boxes indicating your relative promise or standing in relation to each of these qualities:

- Intellectual ability
- Ability to empathize
- Written and oral communication skills
- Aptitude for research

- Leadership
- Capacity for analytical thought
- Capacity for creative thought
- Potential to successfully undertake graduate work
- Ability to work under pressure
- Ability for independent work
- Ability for collaborative work

These are just a few of the categories your professor has to mull over, so you can see that recommending a student is a significant commitment and requires knowing the person and being invested in his or her welfare and future.

❖ TO WAIVE OR NOT TO WAIVE: THAT IS THE OPTION

Every recommendation form requires that a student indicate whether he or she waives the right to see the letter of recommendation. There will be a box for you to check indicating that you do (or do not) waive your rights, and it is important to know why this issue matters and what, exactly, it means. When you waive your rights you are agreeing to relinquish your right to see the letter. By doing so, you demonstrate that you are fully confident about your recommender's comments. Forms with the waived box checked carry more weight with the admissions committee because the implications are understood: this professor could write whatever he or she wanted to without the student having the right to see it. You should WAIVE YOUR RIGHT TO SEE THE LETTER. If you have doubts about what a professor has to say about you, then ask someone else. It's that simple. Refusing (or forgetting!) to waive your right sends the wrong message. It indicates that you are concerned or suspicious about what the professor might say, and for that reason you are reluctant to let the form go out the door sight unseen. It suggests you prefer to satisfy your curiosity over respecting the confidence of your faculty member's appraisal. If you can't waive (your rights), don't ask (for a letter).

However, sometimes students interpret waiving their rights to mean a hands-off policy regarding letters of recommendation. Nothing could be further from the truth. The truth is that you can—and should—have LOTS of input into what goes into your letter, and there is absolutely no reason for you to relinquish your interests in influencing what it contains. Let's turn to that important issue now.

❖ HOW TO MAXIMIZE THE IMPACT OF YOUR LETTERS

When professors agree to write you a letter of recommendation, they are telling you that they value you and they respect you enough to vouch for your success in graduate school. By agreeing to write a letter for you, they are making both a commitment and a significant time investment, as well.

When we write letters of recommendation for our students, we spend, on average, two hours per letter. That's the time it takes to review the materials, draft and revise a letter, fill out all the recommendation forms, print, sign, and send. Multiply those two hours by the number of schools to which each person is applying, and the number of students for whom we write letters, and the total is staggering. Just the two hours alone is about the same amount of time it takes to conduct a dissertation defense or to complete a professional review of a manuscript, and faculty take your letter just as seriously as they do those other tasks.

Knowing the effort involved in writing a letter of recommendation can be quite helpful to you. For one thing, it tells you that your recommender is going to be your advocate, looking for the things to say about you that will maximize the likelihood of your gaining admission in the program of your choice. In other words, they are in your corner and committed to your success. Although it is conceivable that a professor would intentionally write you a lukewarm letter, it is much more likely that he or she would decline to write on your behalf. In our experience, a lukewarm letter more likely occurs by default rather than by design. So let's talk about why that is and how you can prevent so-so letters from occurring.

❖ TURNING A LETTER FROM LUKEWARM TO RED HOT

When professors sit down to write letters, they try to recall everything about you that might be helpful. But memory is selective and fallible, and neither of those features serves your best interest. We are often surprised, even when we write letters for some of our all-time favorite students, how much we forget about them and recall only when prompted. For example, we might know that Susie K. works in our laboratory on social persuasion right now, and that she started last semester, but we forget that she took our Social Psychology course last fall semester, that she participated in the undergraduate research forum last spring, and that she took our General Psychology class more than two years ago. These recollections all fall prey to the *recency effect*.

Of course, *Susie* remembers all of those things but, given that we have had hundreds of students across that time, many of them in large classes, we don't remember that unless she reminds us.

Now we come to the part that counts: you must remind us! How best to do this? Well, it's simple: provide us with a *Thumbnail Sketch*. Let's talk about what should go on the Thumbnail Sketch and how it differs from your vita or personal statement.

❖ THE THUMBNAIL SKETCH

The Thumbnail Sketch serves multiple purposes. As a memory device, it triggers all sorts of recollections for your letter writers. It also provides specific, targeted information that allows them to write a letter more easily, efficiently, and effectively, with more detailed information. Here's how it works, and why.

Without a Thumbnail Sketch, your letter writers sit down and wonder how, exactly, to do what they have promised—write you a strong, detailed letter that contributes to the Gestalt. They try to remember how they know you, the contexts in which they have seen you work, and how that dimly recalled information relates to your particular interests in graduate study. From personal experience, we can tell you that it's almost impossible to come up with something to say without concrete facts to work from. Fortunately, The Thumbnail Sketch provides everything a letter writer needs, and it does it in a simple and straightforward way.

The Thumbnail Sketch fits on one side of a single sheet of paper, nothing more. Think of it as the "executive summary" of your key skills and of your professors' experience with you. Your goal is to make it short and sweet, accessible, and useful. Here's what it contains:

Name and Contact Information

At the top of the Thumbnail Sketch, your name and contact information (phone number and e-mail address) should appear. If your letter writer needs to reach you with questions or to request additional information, you want that contact information to be readily accessible. That information should be followed, in order, by (1) your graduate school objective, (2) a listing of the specific contexts in which you have interacted with your professor, (3) a listing of targeted experiences or skills that you specifically want mentioned in your letter, and (4) a listing of any awards, honors or recognitions that you have received. Let's discuss each of these in turn.

Graduate School Objective

What kind of graduate programs are you applying to? That information appears below your name and contact information. Are you applying to PhD programs in counseling psychology, PsyD programs in clinical psychology, doctoral programs in social, developmental, or cognitive psychology? Are you applying to forensics psychology programs, or to industrial–organizational programs? Are you applying to master's degree programs in general experimental psychology, or in clinical or counseling psychology?

This information is important because, unless you say otherwise, faculty may assume you are applying to the same kind of graduate program that they themselves completed. And this assumption makes sense. If you worked for two semesters in a developmental psychology research laboratory, it's only natural that your developmental professor would assume that you are pursuing graduate work in that area. But what if you are interested in a more applied program that incorporates developmental aspects, such as a child–clinical or marriage and family therapy program? You need to make that information clear. Similarly, you may have worked with a faculty member in clinical psychology, and he or she might naturally assume that you are applying to PhD programs in clinical psychology. But what if you are applying to PsyD programs instead? You need to specify this fact so that you're not inadvertently recommended for a "PhD program in clinical psychology." This sort of misstep can be quite deflating for the admissions committee (to say nothing of the applicant!) who is left wondering about the applicant's genuine interests. A simple line on your Thumbnail Sketch that reads, "Objective: PhD program in clinical psychology" clarifies everything and prevents unwanted confusion.

Previous Contexts in Which You Have Worked Together

Next comes a listing of experiences you have had with your letter writer. Perhaps you took a class or two from that professor, and those can be listed. Maybe you served as a research assistant, an officer in Psi Chi when the letter writer was the faculty advisor, or interacted at departmental talks, during office hours, or in other contexts. Perhaps you wrote an outstanding paper, did a memorable presentation in class, or even conducted an independent study or a senior honors thesis under his or her direction. The point is to list *all* contexts in which that professor has known you and can comment on your work. Each of those will trigger some type of neuronal firing, which will bring back memories of you and your work and help your recommender add content and substance to your letter. Short, simple, and straightforward, this list of prior experiences serves as quick memory cue that makes the job easier for your letter writer and far more effective for you.

Targeted Experiences and Skills

Sometimes students think that, because they have already given their professors copies of their vitas, there is no need for the Thumbnail Sketch. Although your vita may in fact contain all the pertinent information, a Thumbnail Sketch allows you to choose the specific information you would like emphasized. You retain control. You decide what is most important. And, by putting it in short, accessible form on your Thumbnail Sketch, you maximize the chance that your letter writer will wind up including that information in your letter.

What counts as "targeted skills and experiences"? This depends on the kind of programs to which you are applying. If you are applying to research-oriented doctoral programs, you will want to list your research courses (e.g., Research Methods, Statistics, independent study, senior thesis, professional presentations, publications). If, on the other hand, you are applying to more professionally oriented programs, you may want to note your community service and your volunteer work, too. Remember, your goal is always to maximize the goodness of fit between you and the programs to which you are applying. Listing your valuable experience at the child protection agency, for example, might be vital if you are applying to a child–clinical or forensics psychology program, but such experience will have little value if you are applying to a psychobiology or cognitive program. So consider the background and skills that fit with the graduate programs of interest to you, and put that information here in your Thumbnail Sketch.

Awards, Accomplishments, and Recognitions

In this part of the Thumbnail Sketch you simply list your accomplishments. Your GPA (overall, last two years, and in the major) can be included here, as can your GRE scores. But maybe you also were on the president's honor roll, the dean's list, or received a scholarship of some sort. Perhaps you were recognized for your campus work, your excellence in leadership or service, or were otherwise singled out as the recipient of an award or honor of some sort by your department or college. These are all important accomplishments, and your making note of them increases the likelihood that they will be remarked on by professors writing your letters of recommendation. Such comments can be even more powerful than a simple listing on the vita, because they say "this student's accomplishments are significant"—which is, after all, what you hope will be said.

Here is an example of what a Thumbnail Sketch might look like:

Tom Collins
tcollins@unf.com

Objective: To gain admission into a PhD program in clinical psychology (with an emphasis on working with children)

Contexts in which I have worked with you:

- I took your Social Psychology course in the fall of last year and made an A.
- I took your Research Methods course last semester and made an A in the class and on my project, "Social Persuasion in Clinical Contexts."
- I participated in your laboratory on Attitude Change and Social Influence this semester.
- You are supervising my senior thesis on "Social Influence in Clinical Contexts" (expected completion: next term).
- I was fourth author on the poster "Attitude Change in Risky Behaviors Among Late Adolescents" that was presented at the annual meeting of the Southeastern Psychological Association in March of this year.

Selected Experiences and Skills

- Proficient in SPSS, Excel, and Microsoft Access
- Participated in undergraduate research forum, last spring term
- Volunteered at the Crisis Center for the last three semesters (ongoing)
- Volunteered in pediatric intensive care unit at hospital

Awards, Accomplishments, and Recognitions

- Overall GPA = 3.6 (3.7 in the last two years; 3.8 in psychology)
- GRE = 1210 (620 Verbal; 590 Quantitative)
- President's honor roll (all four years)
- Recognized as "Outstanding Volunteer" by the Crisis Center this year
- Elected President of Psi Chi (current)
- Elected Vice President of Psi Chi (last year)

One final note about Thumbnail Sketches: they should be short. In a single glance, your recommenders can see everything about you that is key and can easily integrate (or cut and paste) this information into your letter. Moreover, the Thumbnail Sketch provides details about how your letter writer knows you, and it selectively provides what you consider the most relevant information so that your letter writer doesn't have to make that decision for you. Remember, it's up to you to establish the goodness of fit between your experiences and skills and the programs to which you are applying. Don't worry about redundancy in your letters of recommendation. Having several faculty note selected aspects of your experiences and accomplishments adds additional power and credence to them.

Armed with your Thumbnail Sketch, your letter writer will be able to write a much more effective letter. Consider two faculty members who feel similarly positive about a given graduate applicant. One of them is working from memory, and the other is equipped with a Thumbnail Sketch. Here is what someone *without* a Thumbnail Sketch might say:

Dear Admissions Committee:

John Roberts has asked that I write a letter of recommendation supporting his application for graduate school, and I am happy to do so. John was a student in my Abnormal Psychology class last semester. He also worked with me previously in our social persuasion and attitude-change laboratory. Based on my ongoing interaction with him in the classroom and the laboratory, I am confident that John has the conceptual and research skills necessary to contribute successfully to his program of study and, one day, to the profession of psychology, as well.

His performance in my class and laboratory is consistent with his broader performance here at the university. I understand that John has an outstanding GPA and strong GREs, so I would expect that he would excel similarly in his graduate coursework, fulfilling his outstanding academic promise.

Many of the same qualities that distinguish John's performance in the laboratory and the classroom also extend to the professional domain. He has been actively involved in a number of different service-related capacities, both within the university and outside it. He is a motivated and dedicated individual who takes responsibility and initiative in relation to his professional growth and development.

(Continued)

(Continued)

> In short, I recommend John Roberts to you highly and without reservation. Feel free to contact me if I can provide any additional information in support of his consideration.
>
> Sincerely,
>
> George Burns, PhD
> Professor of Psychology

However, here is a recommendation *with* a Thumbnail Sketch; note the difference!

> Dear Admissions Committee:
>
> John Roberts has asked that I write a letter of recommendation supporting his application for graduate school, and I am happy to do so. John was a student in my Abnormal Psychology class last semester. He also worked with me for three consecutive semesters in our social persuasion and attitude-change laboratory. In that lab, John expressed interest in applying the Elaboration Likelihood Model of attitude change to therapeutic contexts, an innovative idea which represents a potentially important context for extending the application of that theory. Three weeks later, he produced an annotated bibliography of some 40 sources that allowed me to take the first step in the project I then asked him to join. Based on my ongoing interaction with him, I am confident that John has the conceptual and research skills necessary to contribute successfully to his program of study and, one day, to the profession of psychology, as well.
>
> His performance in my laboratory and class are consistent with his broader performance here at the university. His overall GPA of 3.5 is outstanding, and his GPA in the major (3.8) and in his last two years (3.7) demonstrates his exemplary performance within our scientifically oriented major, specifically in the context of other demanding upper division work. His accomplishments are also consistent with his strong GRE score (1250), which signals his outstanding academic capacity.
>
> Many of the same qualities that distinguish John's performance in the laboratory and the classroom also extend to the professional domain. He has served as a telephone hotline counselor for the last year, for example, following his successful completion of an extensive training program in crisis intervention. He also served as a Peer Counselor in the department,

> working to help undergraduates develop clarity about their career plans and develop coursework that would support those interests. His involvement in a number of other volunteer capacities, including Habitat for Humanity and our local homeless shelter, speak directly to his commitment to the welfare of others.
>
> In short, I recommend John Roberts to you highly and without reservation. Feel free to contact me if I can provide any additional information in support of his candidacy.
>
> Sincerely,
>
> George Burns, PhD
> Professor of Psychology

As is clear from this example, both letters praise John, and both are favorable, but the second is by far the better letter. Why? Because, although the first letter employs a number of superlatives, the writer is leaning heavily on generalities and expectations. On the other hand, the writer of the second letter is able to refer to specifics. The concrete examples provided are vivid proof that the professor does in fact know John well. Highly specific letters indicate that the professor values you enough to look for and incorporate the details of your accomplishments into his or her letter. Furthermore, the attention to specific instances and examples allows members of the admissions committee to identify how, exactly, John's experiences and skills might apply to their own graduate program. Finally, more detailed letters are more memorable; when we think back about John, we not only are left with a generally favorable impression but also a range of specific details that help us anchor and recall the basis for that impression.

To recap:

- Look around as early as possible so that you identify courses and professors *before* you need letters of recommendation rather than *at the moment* you need them.
- Cut yourself from the pack. Students take psychology courses for all kinds of reasons. Make sure that you and your interests are known to the professor *during the course.*
- To accomplish the preceding, go to office hours and stay in contact with your professors after the course has ended; if you do

these things, you are in a position to ask the professor, not the TA, for a letter of recommendation.
- Once you're ready to present the professor with the forms, make SURE you have completed all of the information that you are asked to provide *before* giving the forms to your professor. Incomplete forms do not reflect favorably on you, and they make additional work for faculty members who must return the forms to be completed, get them back, and start all over again. There is nothing more deflating than discovering a batch of incomplete forms. What do you suppose the professor will have to say about your ability to undertake graduate work if you have not followed the directions in completing your forms? Because this warning is worth repeating, we will repeat it again and again: *Professors are busy people; do anything and everything that you can to make their jobs easier for them.*

❖ TIMING

Students want to know not only *whom* they should ask for letters but also *when* to ask for them. How far in advance should you ask someone to write on your behalf? The short answer is that it is never too early to ask for a letter of recommendation. Right after the course ends, for example, you could ask the professor if he or she would be willing to write a letter of recommendation. You might say something along the lines of "I was wondering if you would be willing to write a strong letter of recommendation for me. I'm applying to graduate schools next fall and would need the letters, plus the required forms, to be sent out then." If you get a resounding "yes" from your professor, you could reply, "Great! I'll be checking back in with you and getting you everything by the middle of the semester if that's all right. Thanks very much. I appreciate it."

The important point is that you ask well in advance and that you don't return to a professor several semesters (or years!) later to ask for a letter. When you get a positive reply, you provide a timeline and an expectation about when the professor will hear from you and a clear indication that you will provide everything needed to write the letter. You can also offer to meet with the professor, if that would be helpful. For example, you might say, "I'd be happy to meet with you to talk about my graduate school plans, too, if that would be helpful to you in writing the letter. Again, I appreciate your willingness to write a recommendation for me."

❖ PUTTING IT ALL TOGETHER

Once you have written your Thumbnail Sketch, it should accompany your vita, personal statement, and all your recommendation forms to your letter writers. Keep in mind that each of your recommendation forms will require that you fill in your name and the name of your letter writers, as well as indicate your willingness to waive your right to see your letter of recommendation (see "To Waive or Not to Waive: That Is the Option" section). It is essential that you double check to verify that you have completed these parts of your forms.

❖ MAKE IT EASY

To help make things easier, prepare a packet for each professor who has agreed to recommend you. This packet, a collection of essential materials, testifies to your organizational abilities. It also is a courtesy to the people writing on your behalf. For both reasons, take it seriously. Your packet, which is assembled in a folder of some sort, should contain the following:

1. *A list of schools, with complete addresses*—the ones that appear on the envelopes you also supply—along with deadlines, with the most immediate first, and complete information regarding whether forms have to be completed and sent along with the letter. Sometimes the schools will ask for all this material to be returned to the applicant, who then mails it in with the application. In this case, the professor will return the letter and the completed form (if any) to you, sealed, with his or her name written across the flap of a departmental letterhead envelope to ensure confidentiality. The list you create for each professor will look like this:

University of the Americas Department of Graduate Studies in Psychology 1234 College Avenue, Suite 18 Nebraska, Illinois 23456	Deadline: September 18 form and letter sent to dept
University of Gainesville Department of Psychology, Graduate School 14 West Palm Street Miami, Florida 34567	Deadline: October 1 letter only, sent to dept

The Fisher School of Professional
  Psychology
789 Columbia Road
Charlestown, West Virginia 45678

Deadline: October 1
form and letter back to me

Dr. Lillian Smith, Director of
  Graduate Studies
The Institute for Psychological
  Research
University of Londonshire
45 Worcestershire Lane, Northwest
London, England

Deadline: October 15
form only, sent to dept

University of Las Vegas
Department of Graduate Studies
Psychology Department
Box 8856
Las Vegas, Vermont 78901

Deadline: November 1
letter only, back to me

University of the Desert
Psychology Department,
  Graduate Coordinator
P.O. Box 66890
Tucson, Arizona 50392

Deadline: November 5
form only, sent to dept

From this imaginary list you can see how important organization is. The professor has to get letterhead envelopes for two schools: (1) The Fisher School and (2) the University of Las Vegas. The Fisher School requires a completed form, along with a letter, to be included in that sealed and signed envelope returned to the student, whereas the University of Las Vegas requires only the letter. Of the remaining four schools, one requires both a form and a letter, two require just a form, and one requires just a letter. Of course, because some schools want letters to be submitted electronically, the process can become even more complex, especially if a professor is writing on behalf of many students! By being crystal clear about deadlines and what needs to be sent where, you will help enormously in expediting the writing and sending of various combinations of materials to different schools.

2. *Include addressed envelopes* for the schools requesting that materials be sent directly to them. Make sure you attach postage with a paper clip, and make sure that the return address is the university you attend, not your personal address. Why? Because if, for some reason, the letter is returned, it would then go to your home address, as written in the upper left hand corner of the envelope. But you have waived your right to read the letter. Therefore, if the letter is returned, it should go to the person who wrote it—the professor, at the address of the department. So put the professor's name and address in the upper left hand corner of the envelope. Arrange the envelopes in order of their deadlines—that is, the envelope for the program with the earliest deadline should be on top, and so forth.

3. *Include all the forms, and check again before you pass them along to the professor to make sure you've completed the required information.* As mentioned earlier, there isn't much that will dampen the enthusiasm a professor has for you as finding incomplete forms or information that necessitates getting back in touch with you.

4. *Include a copy of your Thumbnail Sketch, your vita, and your personal statement.*

5. *Do not include your transcripts.* Remember, this packet is intended to help the professor to write your letter of recommendation more efficiently and effectively. Your attention to detail and organization are significant contributors in this regard. Little details make a big difference when a professor undertakes writing letters for several students, each of whom is applying to a dozen or so different graduate programs. Those details make a big difference to admissions committees, too, who look for specifics in order to determine the basis for a faculty member's appraisal, to help anchor a memory of the applicant, and to distinguish one applicant from the other.

6. *Write thank-you notes* once all the dust has settled and you are awaiting an interview (be sure to watch the actual interview in *The Online Advisor* for tips)—or an acceptance. These individuals have taken the time to support you and write a letter of recommendation on your behalf. And you never know when you may need another letter from them in the future, so be sure to show your appreciation to them now!

To recap:

1. Ask professors, not TAs, if they would be willing to write you a strong letter, and ask well ahead of time. Tell the professor when you expect to apply to graduate school and when you would need the letter.

2. Prepare packets that contain the following:
   - Complete forms and addressed envelopes
   - Directions to the professor for assembling forms and letters (are they being returned to you or sent directly to the schools?)
   - Deadlines, with the first due date listed first
   - Thumbnail Sketch, vita, and personal statement

FEATURE

Q & A: Letters of Recommendation

Q: Can I include a fourth letter of recommendation if I would like to?

A: Sometimes there are compelling reasons to have an additional letter of recommendation. Remember, though: there is a fine line between letters of recommendation and "fan mail," so make sure that any additional letter speaks to distinctive aspects of your experience that the other letter writers can't address. And you can always add people to your list of references at the bottom of your vita, too, as a way to reflect their input without having them write a letter.

Q: Do all my letter writers have to be psychology professors?

A: Ideally; however, in some cases you may have an English professor, for example, extol your writing skills or your critical thinking skills, or a statistics professor testify to your data analysis ability. If you volunteered at a crisis center, domestic violence center, hospital, or geriatric center, one of your supervisors might be able to say something distinctive about you. The important point is that letter writers should provide information relevant to the programs you are applying to. If possible, recommenders should have doctoral degrees and some experience with writing letters for graduate schools, too!

Q: Can I have a TA write a letter for me?

A: Yes and no. It would be better to see whether your TA could draft a letter that his or her major professor (a PhD) could cosign. That way you get the best of both worlds: the appraisal of someone who has worked very closely with you in one or more contexts (the TA) and someone in a position to evaluate you authoritatively (the professor). Be sure to reread what we say about this subject at the beginning of the chapter, too!

Q: Do I have to waive my right to see my letters of recommendation?

A: Yes. The need to satisfy your curiosity should not trump the value associated with preserving confidentiality. If your letter writers cannot speak about you in confidence, then your reviewers may discount what they have to say. And if you really have concerns about what your letter writers might have to say about you, you might do well to find other letter writers.

Q: Graduate schools all seem to have different deadlines. Can I give my letter writers materials for the schools to which I am applying first, and then give them the other programs with later deadlines as those deadlines approach?

A: No. Give them everything on one list at one time. The chances of confusion and error increase with each new batch of applications that a writer receives. Plus, it makes for a lot more work. It is better for you to bear that burden than for your recommender to bear it. You are the one asking for a favor, remember?

5

Getting Into the Flow

❖ ❖ ❖

Applying for graduate study in psychology is a process, not an event. It's like moving. Yes, there is an actual day when the truck gets loaded and leaves town, headed to your new destination. But before that actual moment when life changes dramatically, there are things to sort through (what to take, what to leave), boxes to pack (carefully), and directions to map out, too. Getting into graduate school in psychology is a lot like that. In order to complete your application you will have to sort through what matters and what doesn't; you will have to carefully package what you view as the most valuable pieces of your experiences, skills, and interests; and, of course, you will need to know where, exactly, you intend to go.

We hope *The Virtual Advisor* serves as a useful guide to you in this regard, wherever you are in the process of your preparation for graduate school. Both *The Virtual Advisor Online Companion* (http://www.thevirtualadvisoronline.com) and *The Pocket Companion* can help you locate where you are in the process and identify ways to make effective headway in the direction of your preferred destination. The attached flowcharts give you some idea of the overall process of graduate school preparation. We discuss each of the components in these charts in greater detail in the final module of your online program, but we want to emphasize two things here.

First, locate on the chart where you currently see yourself as being—a second-, third-, or fourth-year student—but remember, these charts are only a general guide. They help you determine a direction to take, based on your current position, and the ground ahead of you that you still have to cover. If you are like most students, you will find that you have done a combination of things—a bit from this year, a bit from that year—without necessarily making systematic progress down or across any one of the charts. In other words, you may find yourself "between" the charts, and that's fine. The important point is that you can identify terrain that you still need to traverse and that you make some signposts for yourself to help navigate your way through this territory. If you are a sophomore (or junior), for example, these might be reminders such as "Introduce yourself to your professors," "Go to office hours," "Look into Psi Chi," or "Check out possible volunteer work or research opportunities." If you are a senior (or a junior), your list might include things such as "Take (or retake) the GRE," "Contact possible graduate schools," or "Update my vita and draft a personal statement." Wherever you are in the process, remind yourself that because you now know how best to proceed, it's going to be a lot easier to finish. We've had many students who have headed into senior year with little or no explicit preparation and do a great job of catching up as soon as they recognize what, exactly, remains to be done. You can, too.

Second, most students who are applying to graduate school in psychology have little or no explicit preparation for the process. They have completed their coursework, have good grades, have some extracurricular experiences, and then they take their GREs and apply. In other words, they assume that because they have done well as undergraduates, they are likely to be admitted into graduate school, too. Some students are right, of course, but all of them would have benefited immensely by being guided through the process of preparing themselves and their application materials in a more deliberate, systematic way. You, on the other hand, now have an insider's perspective. With *The Virtual Advisor* as your guide, you have been able to map the terrain ahead and get a behind-the-scenes look at the processes and procedures associated with graduate application, so you will be much better informed, and your application will be easier to complete as a result. And as you move through each step in your development, consult your *Virtual Advisor (Online Companion, Pocket Companion,* or both) a second (or third) time. After all, not everyone hears everything an advisor says the first time around!

And that's the point of *The Virtual Advisor*. So rest easy: you don't have to do everything. If you attend to even a small percentage of what we have suggested, you will be way ahead of the pack. You will find yourself passing otherwise talented, capable, and qualified applicants as you move toward your destination, simply because they will not have had the same type of guidance. So we hope you keep your *Virtual Advisor* tucked into your backpack or downloaded onto your iPod and that you will feel free to bring it out whenever you feel lost or in need of further directions. *The Virtual Advisor* is your constant travel companion, and we wish you success along the way, both with your journey and with your destination!

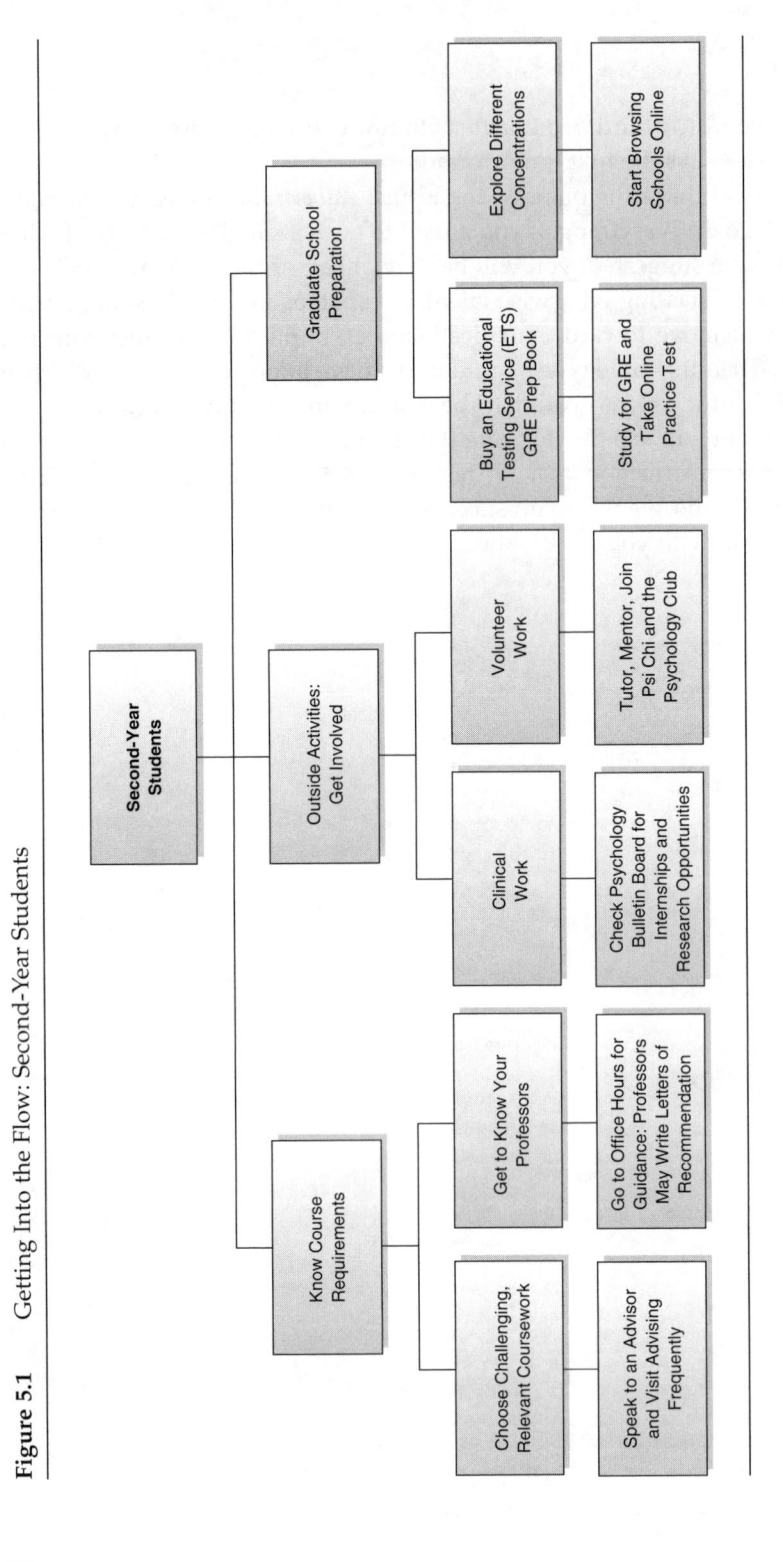

Figure 5.1 Getting Into the Flow: Second-Year Students

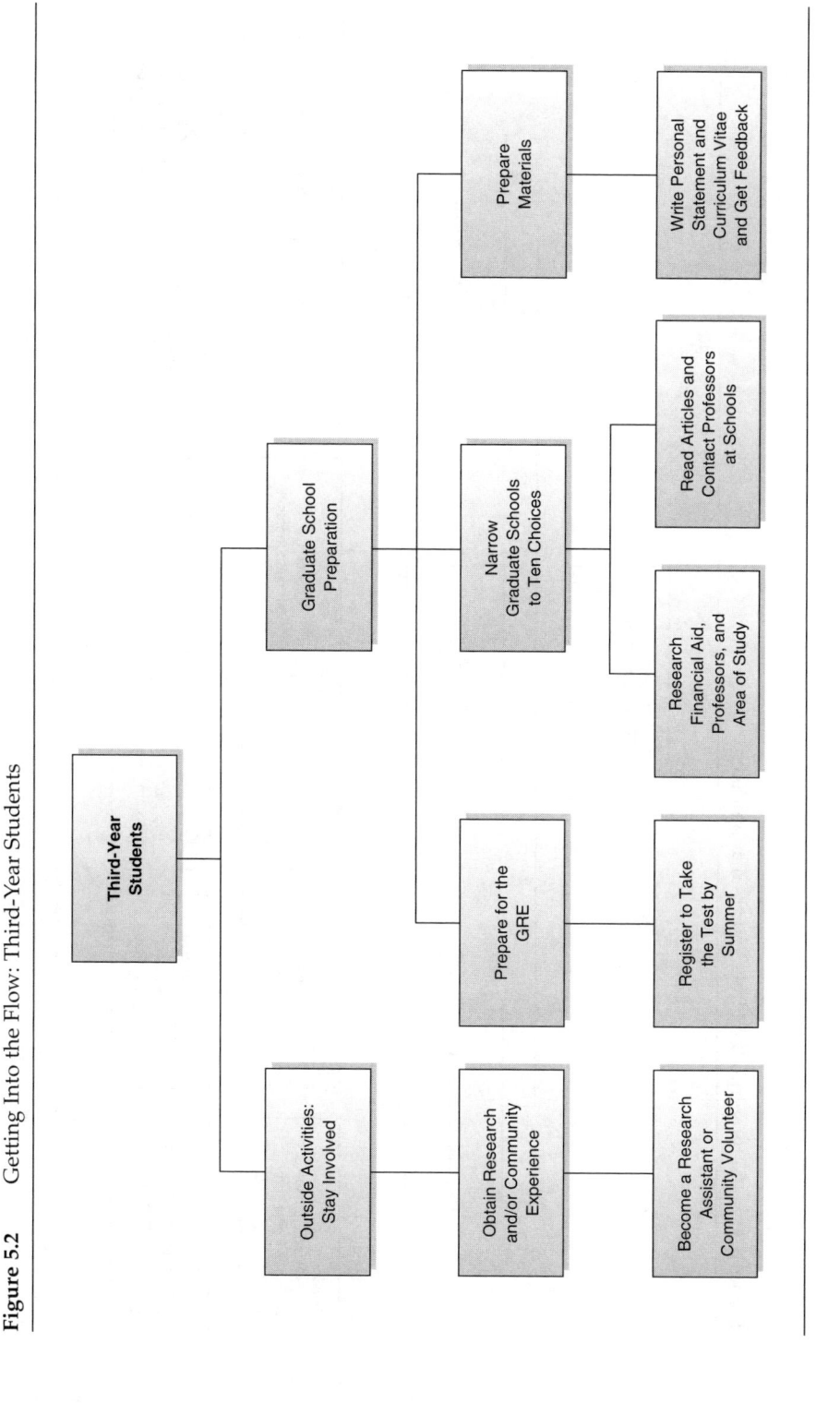

Figure 5.2 Getting Into the Flow: Third-Year Students

Figure 5.3 Getting Into the Flow: Fourth-Year Students

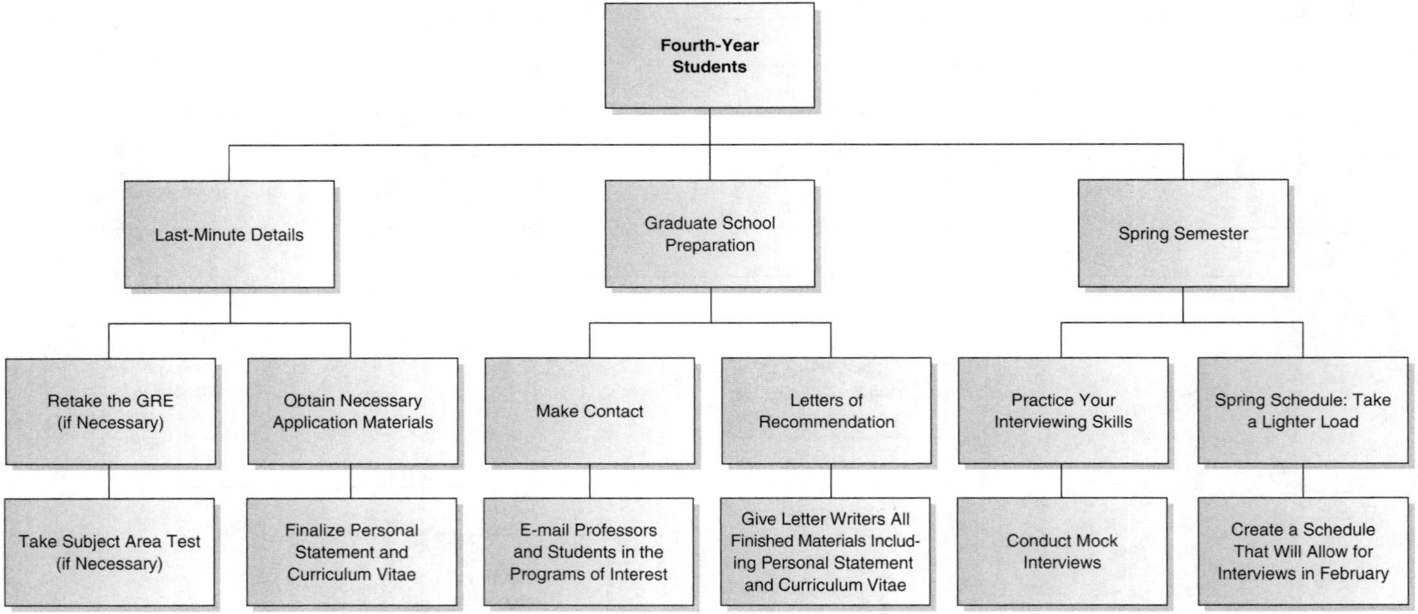

About the Authors

Greg J. Neimeyer, PhD, is Professor of Psychology in the Department of Psychology at the University of Florida in Gainesville. Dr. Neimeyer has served as Graduate Coordinator in the department and as the Director of Training in its American Psychological Association (APA)–approved doctoral program in counseling psychology. He has served as the Chair of the Executive Board of the Council of Counseling Psychology Training Programs in the United States, and has been recognized by the APA as the recipient of its award for Outstanding Achievement in Career and Personality Research. Much of his work focuses on aspects of postmodern psychology and psychotherapy. Elected as a Fellow of the APA, Dr. Neimeyer has also been recognized for his outstanding teaching by Psi Chi, the University of Florida, and by the Golden Key National Honor Society, and he has been inducted into the Academy of Distinguished Teaching Scholars. As a recipient of the University of Florida Outstanding Mentoring Award, he continues to teach and train undergraduate and graduate students in psychology. He also maintains an active clinical practice through his affiliation with the Department of Community Health and Family Medicine at the University of Florida, where he conducts research and workshops on graduate school preparation.

Diane Stevenson, PhD, is the editor of two volumes of Carl Hiaasen's collected columns, *Kick Ass* and *Paradise Screwed*, as well as the coauthor of a grammar text. Currently, she teaches Communicating Psychological Science in the Psychology Department at the University of Florida, where she has also been the Director of the Summer Bridge Program and Reading Coordinator in the Reading and Writing Center. Dr. Stevenson served as the faculty advisor to the University of Florida's chapter of Psi Chi, which named her Professor of the Year, and has been a McNair Mentor, a Minority Mentor, and a Women's Leadership Council Mentor.

BF
77
.N45
2008

Neimeyer, Greg J.

The virtual advisor.

$78.95

35010000551349

DATE			

BAKER & TAYLOR